The Material Girl

What You Wear Can't Conceal Who You Are

MUDIWA NOEL

Copyright© 2017 Mudiwa Noel

All rights reserved. No part of this publication may be reproduced, distributed, or transmitted in any form or by any means, including photocopying, recording, or other electronic or mechanical methods, without the prior written permission of the publisher, except in the case of brief quotations embodied in critical reviews and certain other noncommercial uses permitted by copyright law. This is a work of nonfiction. Some names have been changed.

Published by Mudiwa Noel Enterprises

Unless otherwise indicated, Scripture quotations are from the New King James Version®. Copyright©1982 by Thomas Nelson. Used by permission. All rights reserved.

Scripture quotations marked MSG are taken from *THE MESSAGE*, copyright© 1993, 1994, 1995, 1996, 2000, 2001, 2002 by Eugene H. Peterson. Used by permission of NavPress. All rights reserved. Represented by Tyndale House Publishers, Inc.

Cover Design and Publishing Coordination by Brown & Duncan Brand, BandDBrand.com

ISBN: 978-0-9992023-3-3

Printed in the United States of America

Dedication

This book is dedicated to my good friend Torrean Lynnae Rich #RichGirl…

Torrean was a beautiful person with a BIG heart. She became my friend because of her dedication and persistence to live her life boldly, unapologetically, and based upon God's word. She was the first friend I had who brought me closer to God and helped me welcome His presence in my life. I am unsure if my journey would look like it does today if it wasn't for her guiding me, showing me, and loving me. Sometimes you don't realize how important someone is in your life until they are no longer there.

I am forever grateful for you and the life you exemplified on earth. Although I may not have told you this, you are one of the main reasons I saw it fit to live my life boldly and openly as a Christian at a young age. So to honor you, I will honor your name through charity and giving because that exemplifies who you were as a person. This book might not have had the same meaning if you were not in my life. So I publicly say thank you and you will always be loved by me! #ForeverRich

Acknowledgements

I first have to say thank you to my God; if none of this makes it to be a big hit, I could care less, because I know I followed His instructions and plans for my life. There is no greater feeling than to know and understand that you are totally in the will of God. Doing what He created me to do is rewarding enough!

Mom, I love and adore you. I would be nothing without you. You have been the one when doors are closed and lights are out who prayed and cried for me. I know without a shadow of a doubt God knew exactly what I needed to mold me to be a GREAT woman. So thank you for taking motherhood seriously and vowing to raise your daughters to be humble, loving, giving, and for being okay with me being MYSELF. I hope this book makes you proud and although it may reveal somethings you never knew about me, LOL, it will still give you the joy of knowing I am who I am partly because of your love and support through my bad decisions and heartbreak. Love you dearly!

To my natural father or daddy as I call him, I love you more than you know. Although we have had a rough ride through life, I know you love me. I didn't understand your logic then but I know that you helped instill discipline and the tenacity to do whatever I set my mind to. You have helped me develop and understand life, emotions, and deal with challenges better and I thank you for it.

To my sisters and brothers, Aaron, Jason, Odell, Amaan, Ebony, Asara, and Isis, thank you for letting me be the baby… for loving me and making sure you set good examples. Even at times teaching me what not to do, through your life experiences. Being transparent, open, and honest has been what I needed to pull me through life. You guys played a pivotal part in the journey I have shared with the world so I love you and thank you for it.

To my pastors, spiritual guides, and the ones whom I adore, Pastors Mike and DeeDee Freeman, you guys have NO CLUE how much your faithfulness and transparency has helped me. If I had not been linked to your church and the word you give every week, I would not be as spiritually mature as I am today. We don't talk on the phone every week or sit down at the same table on a daily basis but the guidance you have shown me through your life has been enough. Because of your "Yes!" to God's purpose for your lives as pastors, I was able to step into my purpose. I am grateful for the sacrifices you have made to lead people, and I love you always!

To Arin, Brelyn, Iris, Rachel, Alicia and Natasha, you ladies have been God sent. Every one of you playing your own vital role in my life and pulling me up to be better than I was yesterday.

Arin, I can go on and on about the spiritual connection we have. God has definitely placed you in my life to guide me in the right direction to go through life together sharing each other's pains and frustrations to ministering to one another to get ourselves out of it. You make it okay for me to be me!

Brelyn your life is enough for me. The example you set at such a young age is remarkable and sharing not only that, but your parents with me, has made my life better. The time you spent to encourage me and push me to get this book out means so much and has made my heart smile.

Iris, whether near or far, you hold a precious place in my heart. I have learned so much from my intellectually witty, and Godly friend. They haven't seen anything yet and what's to come in our connection is purposed by God.

My Rachel and My Leesh, the fight you both have in you is crazy. Thank you for not letting me let this book fall by the wayside. You both constantly sent me messages about writing, and it was well worth it, because it's done. Love you girlies!

Natasha, branding guru, your wisdom and knowledge was desperately needed and your heart to see people win is unmeasurable. Thank you for keeping my project on track and lending your expertise in writing, and your team's expertise in marketing, and design.

Lastly, my close friends and family (you know who you are), some of which have made this book; every one of you have played a part in the journey that have filled these pages. For every phone call or conversation and kind words of advice, thank you. The love and support whether near or far, I appreciate and love you for it.

Contents

Foreword 9
Chapter 1: Who am I? 11
    Reflection: Examine Yourself 19
    Journal 21
Chapter 2: Decision 23
    Reflection: Guiding Light 34
    Journal 36
Chapter 3: Material Girl 37
    Reflection: Purpose is Powerful 45
    Journal 47
Chapter 4: My Material for His Material 49
    Reflection: God's Nuggets 52
    Your Pull List 54
Chapter 5: I Serve Multiple Masters 67
    Reflection: Die Daily 71
    Journal 74
Chapter 6: The Root 75
    Reflection: Killing The Weeds 85
    Journal 88

Chapter 7: My Family Tree ⋯⋯⋯⋯⋯⋯⋯⋯⋯⋯⋯⋯⋯⋯⋯⋯⋯⋯ 89
    Reflection: My past isn't my future, ⋯⋯⋯⋯⋯⋯⋯⋯⋯ 97
    but it explains A LOT!
    Journal ⋯⋯⋯⋯⋯⋯⋯⋯⋯⋯⋯⋯⋯⋯⋯⋯⋯⋯⋯⋯⋯⋯⋯⋯⋯⋯ 98

Chapter 8: Friends No Friends ⋯⋯⋯⋯⋯⋯⋯⋯⋯⋯⋯⋯⋯⋯ 99
    Reflection: You are who you hang around ⋯⋯⋯⋯⋯⋯ 109
    Journal ⋯⋯⋯⋯⋯⋯⋯⋯⋯⋯⋯⋯⋯⋯⋯⋯⋯⋯⋯⋯⋯⋯⋯⋯⋯ 112

Chapter 9: Power ⋯⋯⋯⋯⋯⋯⋯⋯⋯⋯⋯⋯⋯⋯⋯⋯⋯⋯⋯⋯⋯ 113
    Reflection: Your Inner Voice ⋯⋯⋯⋯⋯⋯⋯⋯⋯⋯⋯⋯⋯ 122

Chapter 10: My Helper! ⋯⋯⋯⋯⋯⋯⋯⋯⋯⋯⋯⋯⋯⋯⋯⋯⋯ 127
    Prayer of Salvation ⋯⋯⋯⋯⋯⋯⋯⋯⋯⋯⋯⋯⋯⋯⋯⋯⋯⋯ 133
    Reflection: Wisdom ⋯⋯⋯⋯⋯⋯⋯⋯⋯⋯⋯⋯⋯⋯⋯⋯⋯ 134
    Journal ⋯⋯⋯⋯⋯⋯⋯⋯⋯⋯⋯⋯⋯⋯⋯⋯⋯⋯⋯⋯⋯⋯⋯⋯ 136

Chapter 11: The War Isn't Over ⋯⋯⋯⋯⋯⋯⋯⋯⋯⋯⋯⋯⋯ 137
    Reflection: You're a Champion! ⋯⋯⋯⋯⋯⋯⋯⋯⋯⋯⋯ 142
    Journal ⋯⋯⋯⋯⋯⋯⋯⋯⋯⋯⋯⋯⋯⋯⋯⋯⋯⋯⋯⋯⋯⋯⋯⋯ 146

Proverbs 31 Journal ⋯⋯⋯⋯⋯⋯⋯⋯⋯⋯⋯⋯⋯⋯⋯⋯⋯⋯⋯ 147

About the Author ⋯⋯⋯⋯⋯⋯⋯⋯⋯⋯⋯⋯⋯⋯⋯⋯⋯⋯⋯⋯ 179

Foreword
by: Brelyn Bowman

I want to commend my friend Mudiwa, first for following the passion in her heart and publishing her book, and secondly for being open and transparent about her journey. Transparency is something we often lack in the Christian community. Upon hearing the phrase "material girl," the first inclination is to think negatively because of what the world has created her to be. You may think this girl is stuck up, full of herself, self-seeking, and only after what she can gain in life. However, in this book Mudiwa shares another perspective on what it means to be a material girl, bringing light and life to the meaning. She allows us to see that there's nothing wrong with loving yourself, being all that God created you to be, and having nice things. It's easy to accept society's definition of materialism, but when you have a God-ordained understanding of who you are, you won't fall for the traps, instead you'll rise above every time!

God has a plan for you to prosper, and when you delight yourself in Him then will He give you the desires of your heart. I've personally watched Mudiwa's growth in this particular area of her life. Things weren't always easy coming from the environments she was used to, but as you read her story, you will see how she used those challenges as object lessons to get to where she is today.

Mudiwa shares key principles that will help you begin to see your self the way God sees you. After reading this book, you'll no longer define your life and purpose by things, but by the purpose God has predestined for you.

Chapter 1
Who am I?

I walked out of the bathroom and burst into laughter. "So," he began to question... "What happened? What does it say?" My mind was still processing everything. I could hear each word that came out of his mouth, but I was unable to respond. I was limp, maybe even dead inside, without an ounce of life in me. He asked me again, this time impatient and almost irate at this point. "Maaannn, WHAT DOES IT SAY?" I was still trying to form the words to convey that my life was about to change drastically. Unable to speak a word, I went back into the bathroom, looked down to make sure it was true, and there it was—the proof—a small white stick with two pink lines. I was seventeen and pregnant.

Nothing made sense to me anymore. Up until that point, that day seemed the same as the previous 6,300 and some odd days that I had existed on earth. That day, however, a Saturday that I will never forget, changed my life. I hadn't realized it yet. I was seventeen and pregnant. But I rationalized with myself—*no big deal right? This is common behavior for my generation. A lot of girls my age are careless, or even brainless, and rarely consider what it takes to raise a child. But they still do it.* However, I was asking myself *how did I get here? Why am I here? Is this really happening? And*

The Material Girl

what do I do? Having no one to really talk to, but a bunch of benign teenagers, or let me say young adults, that question seemed impossible to answer, but I continued to try to make sense of this all, at least in my own mind.

It was a beautiful Saturday in March, during my senior year of high school. Spring break was in a few weeks; the countdown to graduation was on, and as usual, I was at my grandmother's home in Southeast D.C. I went out the night before with a girlfriend from school. We hit up the Spring Jam concert that was being held at the Tunnel Nightclub in Washington, D.C. I had not turned eighteen yet, but clubbing was my norm. I had been using my older sister's ID since I was sixteen-years-old. So, this weekend started out the same as a lot of weekends prior to, and I decided to crash at my grandmother's house after the club.

I was straightening up that Saturday morning and I came across a pack of maxi pads. For some reason, seeing them made me realize that I couldn't even recall how long it had been since I had my last cycle. Most girls my age would panic. However, I kept doing what I was doing.

It wasn't until about an hour later when I thought about how annoyed I was with the guy I was dating, Lamont. He had not been very attentive lately, so I decided that in order to get his attention, I'd let him know about missing my period. I didn't really think I was pregnant. I just wanted to get him frazzled. At this point in my life, I was an attention hog, and I wanted everything to revolve around ME. I would often lie to gain attention—little white lies, not any life changing, earth chattering lies. Often they were small enough lies that seemed real, slight twists of the truth. So although I legitimately couldn't remember the last time I had a menstrual cycle, it really didn't bother me because I just knew I wasn't pregnant.

What You Wear Can't Conceal Who You Are

I sat and pondered how I would mention it to him for a few minutes, then I called him and prepared myself for the theatrics. He answered my call on the first or second ring, "Yeah what's up!" In a haughty, yet urgent tone, I responded, "Hey ummmmm you need to come over!"

"Why, what's going on?" He sounded truly perplexed by why I seemed so anxious to have him over. I started to whisper to ensure that my grandmother couldn't hear me. "I need to take a pregnancy test, because I can't remember the last time I came on!"

"WHAT! Okay, I'll be there in a minute." About a half an hour went by, and he came in the house. To my surprise, he had already purchased the test! I thought he would be too embarrassed to go into a store and purchase the test himself, so when I saw the urgency he had for the matter and how fast he had come over, I started to feel uneasy. Maybe it was guilt. Suddenly, I realized this *could be real.* I had picked up a few pounds over the last few weeks, and I had been kind of sluggish; I was eating everything in sight, and I had been sleeping as if I had a 9 to 5. It hit me: maybe I was really pregnant!

He sat at the end of the bed rushing me to take the test. As I continued to clean, he was not visibly anxious, "I mean are you going to take the test or what?" I took my time and eventually responded to him by saying, "I'm about to. If I'm pregnant, me taking it now, versus fifteen minutes from now isn't going to change anything." Truly I was using time as a stalling tactic, because I was beginning to consider the fact that I could really be pregnant. I was in shock, and trying to hide it.

I can remember those next few minutes of my life as if this happened yesterday. It was so surreal and scary. My palms began to sweat; my stomach turned in knots. Ten minutes (which seemed like

The Material Girl

an hour) had passed, so I grabbed the test and headed to the bathroom. I had never taken one of these tests before, so I asked him, "How do I take this thing?" Lamont was two years older than me and he had obviously experienced a similar scare before; He said, "Just pee on the stick!" He was impatient, annoyed, and a tad bit scared of the "what if?" So I read the instructions as I walked into the restroom. Then, I started to pee on the stick and immediately I noticed a line. I thought to myself, *wait is it supposed to happen this fast?* Then I looked at the box and noticed that two lines indicated "pregnant," so I exhaled a small sigh of relief. But then, a moment I had been dreading became a reality. Another line slowly appeared. *Is this really happening,* I thought. I wiped off the stick and placed it on the side of the tub. I sat there stuck, not able to move or speak. Something that I never really considered could happen to me was *actually* happening. The test was positive, and I was pregnant. Unsure of how to tell him, I stayed locked in the bathroom for about two additional minutes just trying to figure out what to say.

    I didn't want to have to tell him, to utter the words which would make this surreal experience real. So instead I laughed. I laughed not because it was a laughing matter. I had just found out that I was carrying a life within me, but I was lifeless, hopeless, and more so, clueless. So I laughed, because I didn't know what else to do. I didn't want to talk about it. I just wanted it all to go away.

    Lamont was totally confused by my response. I guess he didn't know what to say. I had just come out of the bathroom after taking a pregnancy test, and I was laughing. He knew this was no laughing matter. After he asked me for the test results without a response, I finally mustered up enough courage to say, "Go see for yourself!" He looked like a ghost when he came out of the restroom. But me on the other hand, I was still laughing. Not in a hysterical-this is so funny laugh, but in a *ha! this isn't really happening*—shaking-my-head type of laugh. He sat back down on the end of the bed, paused for a minute and said, "You have to get an abortion!"

Wait what? I don't have to do anything! I thought to myself. *I just found out I was pregnant and the first thing you want to talk about is an abortion.* I swear the nervousness left and anger took over my mind and body. I didn't want to bring attention to us, so I kept my tone at a respectful level, but I felt like screaming at the top of my lungs.

I was scared and I didn't know how to say what I was really thinking. "Yeah, I guess so," I responded. He immediately took out his phone, called his mother, and told her what was going on. They spoke in code as if I wasn't sitting there and was not the primary character in this scene that was taking place. I grew furious as they discussed my body and what I was going to do with it, without talking to me. He just ignored me as I sat there confused and hurt, and he assumed what I'd be doing with *my* body.

We were both young and confused, but still I couldn't understand why a guy who had just learned that he was expecting a child would call his mother. I was scared and embarrassed to even utter the words, let alone tell ANYONE, especially my mother. I wasn't getting the attention that I so-badly wanted. I felt alone and abandoned—not only physically, but mentally abandoned. My thoughts didn't matter, my feelings nor my body were considered. As he spoke to his mother, I just sat there. I was so young and in the process of being easily manipulated. I had nothing to say. I was angry, angry that I was in this predicament, angry that he didn't once ask me how I felt about it, angry that this stupid boy got me knocked up, and now he was trying to walk away from this situation as if I would be a disastrous mom. There was no way I could just run to the phone and tell my mom or sisters. I was so embarrassed and confused to even part my lips to tell anyone that I was pregnant. I didn't know much about the abortion procedure, and back then, I didn't have the Internet to give me answers to my endless questions about "abortion." I knew nothing about the risks, nor did I even realize how life-threatening the procedure could have been. I just knew that I didn't want to decide without considering all the possible outcomes. I decided at that point that I would find out everything I needed to know, think about it, and figure out what I wanted to do.

I had a conversation with myself: *"I don't need him or anybody else to raise my child. Life doesn't stop just because I am pregnant. My oldest sister had my niece at eighteen, and she is married and living the good life while raising my niece. Someone will still marry me with a child of my own. You know what, screw him! I don't need him. He can jump off a bridge for all I care."*

Then I snapped out of it. His voice interrupted my thoughts. "Well I'm about to leave. I have some things to take care of. I'll talk to you a little later."

"Okay," I said. I didn't attempt to walk him out. I just returned to my Saturday-afternoon cleaning, and I was glad that he was finally leaving. We didn't say much to each other, and we barely touched. He kissed me goodbye and left. That kiss meant nothing to me. I needed someone to tell me it would be okay and that no matter what I decided to do, they would support me, love me, and help me through this. That's what I needed. Not an empty kiss.

I was so upset. At that moment, I started to hate him. I called one of my best friends, Tara, and told her what had just happened. She was pregnant too and could relate. We talked for hours; she told me what she was going through and how I didn't want to deal with the same thing. We went through all the possible scenarios. What if

What You Wear Can't Conceal Who You Are

I told my mom? What if I didn't? What would my sisters say? Who would help me raise the child? Could I still go to college? We discussed any possible situation that could arise. I tried to cry, but nothing came out. I was so empty and emotionless, and I didn't know how to snap out of it.

So I went back to the bathroom, looked at the test that I had left on the sink, and suddenly looked at my reflection in the mirror. It was almost as if I was gazing into a trick mirror, and I could not recognize the person staring back at me. Unrecognizable, I had never met or seen this girl before, but she was living in my body. So I asked her. "Who are you?" *A mother, a student, a daughter, a friend? Are you caring? Compassionate, a liar, afraid?* "Who are you, and why are you here?"

The real question wasn't, "Who are you?" it was "Who am I?" As I looked in the mirror and saw my reflection, I realized that these simple, yet complex, three words were daunting. I had no clue who I was. I proceeded to ask myself again, "Who am I?" Yet still, no answer. I was still in shock. It was as if I was an infant again and I was still trying to piece together a new language or make something of a new life.

Then I thought, *why can't I just close my eyes, count to ten, and everything go back to normal? How had I been going through life carelessly thinking of no one but myself? Who was I to think that I could do this all alone and not need help from anyone?* Every day was like that song, "It's my party, I can cry if I want to, cry if I want to, cry if I want to. You would cry too if it happened to you!" But at this point, I was not crying. I was not partying. I was standing in the middle of my grandmother's bathroom with an EPT test in hand looking at a girl who I didn't recognize. *Am I happy? Am I even really here? Maybe this is a joke.* I laughed at how stupid I looked in the mirror, so perplexed. I laughed at all of the irrational

The Material Girl

decisions I had made. I laughed because, at seventeen, I had lived life as if it was my stomping ground—doing, having, and being whatever I wanted. I had no care and no concern for anything or anyone if it did not benefit me. Yet, on that March day, I had learned so much just by asking myself the question, "WHO AM I?"

That one moment told me so much about myself. It was the moment that I realized that I really had no clue who I was as a young woman and what I was doing. But contrary to the notion that seventeen-year-olds are irrational, unbothered, immature, and just plain old stupid, I was not stupid. Over the years, I've learned that teenagers are not stupid in the sense that they have no brain power. They just make irrational and stupid decisions. There are more seventeen-year-olds who lack enough life experiences to know completely where they are going or who they are, but they have worked hard for something. They have found a passion and desire and they've stuck to it. Whether it is their education, art, music, or business, there are more teenagers who have it together in our society, than we give them credit for. Sadly, too often we focus on the reckless behavior of some teens, and we have constructed societal beliefs that all young people are that way.

At that moment in my grandmother's bathroom, I made a decision that I didn't want to be a statistic. I was uncomfortable with being mediocre or average, and I would no longer confine myself to the stereotypes of just another young black girl. I would disconnect myself with the world that had become familiar to me. I would finally step up to be the person I knew I was created to be. Since I was a little girl, I knew that I was not ordinary. I was born with extraordinary traits and there was only one me. I always felt like an outsider trying to fit in, but no more. I would no longer allow the popular crowd to dictate my decisions. I decided that I would be me, whoever that was. I would embrace my weird traits and desires.

I would stimulate my mind with information that would propel me to new opportunities and possibilities. I was created to be great and I was going to explore every bit of that greatness. The only issue with this was that I didn't know how I would go about doing it. How was I going to find myself and who would help me?

I knew there was more to life and the world than what I was experiencing. I had no idea what it was, but I sensed that life wasn't over for me just because I was pregnant. My eyes were open to see new possibilities, new trials, and new opportunities. I decided to figure out what that *more* was. I decided, *I am moving on from this situation as a conqueror, and I am not going to change my life's path. I will make my situation work in my favor.*

At that moment, I went blank. For a minute, I had pumped myself up and was ready for war. The only thing that I questioned was *what war was I fighting?* After all that self-motivation and excitement, I looked down and thought about another life. How can I just reach for the stars, make changes to my life when I'M PREGNANT! Reality set in, and I fell on the bed, face wet from tears, I grabbed the pillow next to me and screamed as loud as I could (still careful not to disturb my grandmother). I drifted off to sleep, hoping that when I woke up, I would realize that it was all a dream.

Reflection: Examine Yourself

Life can take you off track and present you with obstacles that you hadn't prepared for. Not allowing the obstacles to consume or overtake you is essential in your growth. The strongest people are the survivors, who not only take the punches, but fight back with a few blows of their own. This situation could have been my crutch. I could have fallen in such a deep state of depression, (pitying my self with toxic thoughts like *I am a failure*), that I could have loss all will to move forward. To the contrary, after getting hit in the face with the consequences to my actions, and imagining reproducing and raising another human being, I was forced to look inward because I felt the weight of that responsibility. I was not ready to provide a stable home for a person who deserved the world. I did not take this potential new life lightly, even at that age, I sensed the severity of it all and how God doesn't bless everyone with this opportunity. Everyone's situation is different. My wakeup call came in the form of a pregnancy. While reading this book, my prayer is that you begin to self-reflect on the events of your life, examine the trials and tribulations you have endured, and consider what you have learned from those experiences. God is always trying to get our attention to pull us closer to Him.

    I pray that my testimony opens your eyes to the things God has for you. God's way is so much better than the life we try to create for ourselves, and it wasn't until I had to make a life altering decision that I realized I didn't have to do life on my own. From this point on, you will see that at the end of each chapter there is a reflection to help you navigate through this book and reflect on how the principles I discuss apply to your own life. In this first entry, I just want you to journal your thoughts after reading my story. How does this relate to you now or in the past? What things have you placed too much attention on and lost yourself. This could be a relationship, a job, or even your own family drama. What things in your life could have the potential to break you? Use these pages to write freely knowing you are reading my journey but beginning to embark on one of your own.

What You Wear Can't Conceal Who You Are

Examining Myself..............................

… The Material Girl

Chapter 2
Decision

We live in an overly sexualized world, and our children are exposed to sex at an early age. As an educator, I overhear stories of students in elementary school experimenting with sexual acts. Working in the school system for over ten years has put me in many predicaments where I have had to talk to my students about the consequences of having sex. They make irrational decisions without considering how those decisions can affect their lives and the lives of the people around them. I have had so many girls get pregnant and show little-to-no remorse for placing the burden of taking care of a child on their parents. They minimize the struggle that comes with caring for a child and assume that because some make it look easy, they too are prepared to care for a child. They fail to realize the cost for daycare is more than they can afford working at McDonalds or Macy's. Nor do they realize that they are less-than-qualified to get a well-paid job with only a high school diploma. This new generation of children go through life feeling entitled to things without having to work hard. The notion that everyone can be a rapper, producer, athlete, model, or even "insta famous" has polluted their minds and overshadowed the real meaning of *hard work pays off*.

The Material Girl

Overtime, I have realized that this issue regarding perception verses reality is often rooted in parents allowing the world to raise their children versus doing the parenting themselves. I am not a biological parent, but have parented so many children through tumultuous situations. Too often, parents choose to opt out of having the sex and or pregnancy conversations with their children. Many parents take the position that if they do not talk about sex, it will go away and their children won't explore the subject matter on their own. To the contrary, if children do not constantly lend their ears to their own parents, they will lend their ears to something or someone else. I work in a high school in the Baltimore School System, and both here, and in urban areas throughout the United States, it has become apparent that a lack of parenting has become an epidemic and root cause to many issues that young people face. My students' parents are around my age, and many of them were brought up in the times when parents didn't talk to their children about sex. I believe this has been a learned behavior.

In my generation, parents and grandparents' generations were not comfortable talking about sex, and so they ignored it until an unwanted pregnancy (or something worst) reared its head. So now, the reality for my students is that their parents' voices are overshadowed by world's views of sex or their parents have avoided the conversation altogether. Sometimes, I really believe that parents today try too hard to give their kids more than what they had that they lose sight of the importance of setting boundaries. Instilling rules and consequences helps children to grow up with an understanding that there are effects of their actions. Most parents condition their children by punishing them through beatings, which last two-to-three minutes, but fail to teach them that consequences are not always temporal. Children learn from their environments. Young people grow up exhibiting the same behaviors they have endured or seen around them.

What You Wear Can't Conceal Who You Are

Understanding these statements can help you to become conscious of how your views of sex have developed. If the only conversation you had with your parents about sex was "just don't do it!" Or, they didn't happen at all until after you had sex, then your perception of sex probably came from the world. This is not uncommon; however, it can be dangerous. The world views sex as something casual, common, and necessary to our everyday lives. But what if I challenged that very notion. Consider that the actual intent of sex was not just to fulfill a natural sensation for pleasure, but to procreate human lives to carry out your family's legacy. The momentary satisfaction can come with a lifetime of pain and our society advertises sex with having the warning and danger that pollutes our young people. I always think of the commercials about new drugs. It is always funny for me to hear the end of the commercials when they outline all the possible dangers that come with taking the medicine. I wonder "do people actually listen to this and still decide to take the meds?"

Then I think to myself what if sex was placed in a commercial with all the disclaimers at the end. Would people still do it as frequently, with multiple partners at a time, or without protection? If the same commercial to promote sex talked about all the great things that come from it like the release of stress, the feeling of pleasure, and the birth of a beautiful child but then that pretty voice came in saying, *"Side effects of sex can prevent your ability to function properly when emotional distraught or overwhelmed due to finding out you have contracted Herpes, Hepatitis, Chancroid, Trichomoniasis, HPV also known as genital warts, Chlamydia, Gonorrhea, Bacterial Vaginosis, Syphilis, Scabies, Pubic "crab" lice, HIV/AIDS or unwanted pregnancies. These STDs and STIs can be passed to your fetus if not properly taken care of by your doctor. Child birth can lead to financial and health challenges, absentee parents, or a child born with disabilities. Do not have sex if under*

The Material Girl

the age of 21, unmarried, and unstable. Please consult or be advised by someone with experience or knowledge in this area before having sex." I run this commercial in my head, and although it sounds bad, I still believe some people will not hear the side effects until it happens to them. Then those people will appear in commercials similar to those for "Don't Smoke!" by the cancer society saying "Don't have sex!" Sex has been and continues to be a lot of people's kryptonite, even my own.

When I was seventeen and pregnant, I thought about how much my decision to keep the baby could affect my entire family, not just myself. However, I did not consider whether or not I was ready to handle the emotions and consequences that came with sex. Nor did I have the proper guidance to avoid becoming pregnant as well as protect myself from the negative outcomes of having sex. I was more focused on my parents finding out I was pregnant than them learning that I was sexually active. Today, I work so hard to protect my students by speaking to them about the consequences that come from engaging in sex. I never start these conversations, but somehow students always come to me for advise in this area. I don't outright say "don't do it!" but I engage them in thought provoking conversations about their responsibility to themselves and their family when making smart choices. I become an ear to hear and a person of good character and judgement. I always lead by example and share with them my own values and beliefs. It saddens me at times because not only is pregnancy an issue, but many young people lack respect for their bodies. They just don't realize how precious they are in God's eyes. I relate, because when I was their age, I didn't realize my worth either.

At one point, I was a sweet young girl caring for everyone and everything around me and I was so sensitive to the needs of others. All that changed by fifth grade. My experience of hurt and rejection, not just from people and the world around me, but from my own father, changed me. I think I could have handled the mocking and bullying by little kids, but I couldn't deal with not feeling loved by both of my parents. Don't get me wrong. My dad had good intentions; he was the disciplinary. He was the one my siblings and I were the most afraid of when we got into trouble. I was such a social child that it was hard for me to remain attentive when I was younger. Because of attention deficit, I was constantly in trouble for my lack of performance in school. My father would praise my sister for her straight A's and in the same breath, tell me to work harder. He would always speak to me about my behavior in school and would often come over to my mom's house just to give me a whooping. I don't think that my father or mother realized how their intentions to discipline me only made me build a wall, so that I could endure feelings of shame and scrutiny. I always tell my friends who are parents to make sure they balance the love with discipline. I do not believe there is a cookie-cutter recipe for raising mentally and physically healthy children, but there is a way to ensure you are providing the best of both worlds. Seeking God's guidance is first and should be the most dominant parenting style of choice. Parents must understand that each child is different and created to do something great on earth. Parents have been deemed worthy of caring for and nurturing the seed inside of their children, and both parents' love is crucial to their development. Video games, music, reality (not so reality) TV, the streets, their friends, or even the church cannot be left responsible for raising children. Parents who understand how important they are to their children's lives will take the time to know what each child needs to live up to their God-ordained purpose.

    I experienced the downfall of mismanaged parenting firsthand. My parents weren't terrible parents to say the least and they did more right than they did wrong. However, I was different and

The Material Girl

needed more time and attention than some of my other siblings. I know that may sound harsh and selfish, and most parents will negate this truth with some concern about showing favoritism. However, as a teacher, I have had to learn that not each child needs the same amount of attention and giving each child what he or she needs versus what I think they need removes the very idea of playing favorites.

By the time I was a teenager, I felt unloved and had developed a wall that made me numb to everyone else's feelings. I was thoughtless and made decisions that I felt would protect me. I focused on what benefitted me and discarded everything else. I didn't care about doing anything for others; I used people for things that I wanted, no matter how it affected them, and I lied when necessary. I hardened my heart so that I wouldn't get hurt. My focus was more on how I looked on the exterior, versus the core of who I was. I figured if people could see the image that I created, I could blend in and if I was lucky, be seen as superior.

To say I was out of touch with reality is an understatement, but what teenager isn't? I didn't realize how out of touch that I was until I came up pregnant. Obvious questions for a teenager in my predicament are, "Don't you know if you have unprotected sex you will get pregnant?" "Why didn't you get on birth control?" These are the same questions I had for myself. Growing up in the late 90s, young pregnancies were not as common as they are today, although most young people were having sex and weren't thinking about saving themselves for marriage. Most of the students that I teach or have taught, have mothers who became pregnant between the ages of seventeen and twenty-one. For me, however, I knew this was not the life I was intended to have, because although my family wasn't perfect, they were extremely old fashion. We never had discussions about not having sex, however I remember being told "don't get pregnant." As a matter of fact, the only time I can remember talking to my mom about sex is when I got caught fooling around in the bathroom with my boyfriend during my eleventh grade year. My dad and I never talked about sex, but we really never talked at all.

After seeing my stomach grow over the next nine to ten weeks, I knew that this baby deserved a better life. At this point, me and the boyfriend were barely even speaking. He had a lot of demons to deal with and growing to do, and so did I. I did not want to raise a child as a single mom, and I feared my child would have self-worth and trust issues, as I did, as a result of the things that went on with my parents as a child. I don't blame my short comings on my mom or dad, but my parents now realize how their actions affected my emotional state.

I was said to be three months pregnant, which I didn't believe. The doctors didn't give me a sonogram; they based this on my last period. I was starting to form a small belly, and I wasn't really trying to hide it. I didn't all of a sudden start wearing baggy clothes, nor did I hide the fact that I was always sleepy and hungry. I just lived life as normal and hoped my parents nor sisters wouldn't notice. At that point, about five of my friends knew that I was pregnant and their polls were divided—some of them told me to keep it, and others were like *'gurl get rid of it.* Nonetheless, I made the best decision that I could for the child, or so I thought. My thinking was that it was way better not to exist than it was to be born and not exist. That's how I felt about myself. I was alive, and yet not existing. I did not have an identity. I couldn't tell the truth from a lie, and I was unable to be honest with myself about who I had become. Before I made the final decision to have the abortion, I wish the me now could have written this letter to myself.

The Material Girl

Dear Mudiwa Noel,

So, what are you going to do now? Fighting for your life and having one inside of you is a tough battle to win. You're dead inside, while you're trying to convince everyone around you that you are winning. You didn't even know the severity of the fight you have been fighting all along. You've been thinking that it was about you this entire time, waltzing through life with no cares. It has caught up with you. I know it sounds harsh, but I know it's the truth, because I am you. I am the one who started this whole thing. I am the reason why you are at this point. I know that you're numb, but that feeling will subside and when it does, the pain will be excruciating. However, I've got some good news! Even though you caused your pain, life isn't over. You can rebuild what is broken and find what is lost. I understand your pain and know your heart. Just confront the demons that you have tried to tuck away. Giving birth can also be a way of experiencing a rebirth of you. Reclaim your own life. It's not too late to change or do the right thing; you just have to look to your Heavenly Father and put on the strength He established just for you over 2,000 years ago, when he gave up the life of His Son so that you wouldn't have to lose your life. You're beautiful, smart, funny, outgoing, intelligent, and a woman of integrity. This one situation does not change who you are and who's you are. Put on the wisdom of God and in all things get understanding, for you are a child of the most high God, who loves despite our infractions. You are and forever will be his beloved and favored daughter.

Love,

Wiser You!

What You Wear Can't Conceal Who You Are

My reality was so misconstrued by seventeen, and it was hard to wrap my head around taking care of another individual. So after all the contemplation and talking it through with my close friends, I decided to abort my pregnancy. It was not an easy decision and I was totally scared out of my mind, but couldn't bear the thought of being bound by motherhood without even knowing who I was. I committed to letting the baby go, but I also committed to letting me live. Looking back, sometimes I wish I made the other choice. Then at other times, I am glad that I made the decision that I did. Now at the seasoned age of thirty-three, with no children, I sometimes wonder if I will ever have kids. I wonder if God is punishing me by not allowing me to have met my husband and if the delay will prevent me from being happily married with two to three kids running around. Will I ever be allowed to bear children because I destroyed a precious gift from God? I battle with these thoughts from time-to-time, but I have learned to fight these thoughts with the word of God to remind myself that He will never leave me nor forsake me, and the promises of God are always yes and Amen. After I became saved and started to deal with these feelings, I would turn to the scripture in **2 Corinthians 5:17**, which reads "Therefore if any man be in Christ, he is a new creature: old things are passed away; behold, all things are become new." This scripture helped me to remember that no matter what my emotions told me, God would always keep me and love me despite my bad decisions. Sometimes however, even when knowing how great He is and the power He possessed, I can't help to feel like maybe I went too far. I know many women who feel this way, women who like me, have made mistakes that they feel have disqualified them from the promises of God. If this you, just return to the words of **2 Corinthians 5:17**. You are a new person in Christ.

The Material Girl

During the spring break of my senior year, I was between eight and ten weeks pregnant and ready to have an abortion. Lamont, who was not much of a boyfriend by that time, made all of the arrangements. He scheduled the appointment for the abortion on the Monday of spring break. He, his mother, and I would go. Why he wanted his mother so involved is beyond me, however, I went with it. I really liked his mother and she was fond of me as well. However, that day she really annoyed me. As I was preparing to do the most nerve-racking thing I had ever done in my life and while I was worrying about everything that could've possibly went wrong, she wanted to make small talk. Among other things, she asked me if my mom knew and if I would to tell her. I wanted to scream. "LADY LEAVE ME THE HELL ALONE!" It was clearly none of her business or concern. She should have been questioning her son as to why he thought it was okay to get me pregnant. So we pulled up, and the place was closed, "HALLELUAH!" That should have been a sign for me not to do it, because the relief I felt knowing it wouldn't happen that day was so refreshing. We left that day to return that Wednesday. This time, his mother was absent, but he brought along his younger brother. I look back and try to figure out why in the hell did this guy bring a support system as if he would be on the table enduring the pain. I had no one. I felt alone, isolated, stupid, and helpless.

I had already known that I needed to be eighteen to have an abortion without my mother's consent, so I brought my sister's ID, the same one I had been using to get into clubs. I signed in and they collected my ID as well as the money to pay for the procedure. The receptionist called me back and started the process. She took my vitals, estimated how far along I was, prepped me, and explained the process. So there I was on the examination table by myself getting ready to go through this alone. Recalling this event makes me think about Jesus and how all the noise stopped when He was strapped to the cross. I'm not at all comparing this to Him dying for my sins, but it's so profound how all the noise stops when you are alone and you endure all by yourself. No one to persuade you out of it or to give you advice. There is nothing or no one, but us and God so what voice is speaking the loudest. YOURS? The one who is clueless and lost in the world or the One who gave you life and a way of escape? I wish I knew what I know now. I wish I would have listened to His way of escape years before getting to this point. I didn't know this Jesus everyone talked about. I had heard He did great things, but no one ever shared with me His true goodness, or maybe they did, and I just wasn't listening at that age.

I was on the doctor's table with my legs sprawled wide open as if I was giving birth, but instead, I was killing the life that God had placed inside of me. Perhaps he did equip me to nurture, cultivate, and grow, but I was unqualified to be a mom. I hadn't yet figured out who I was as a woman. So that day I endured. I endured the pain of the suction machine killing the life formed inside of me, and I really believed it killed a softer side of me that I had become familiar with over the past ten weeks. I did not cry. I did not scream. I grunted my teeth, flinched a little, and fought. I was fighting for my life back from the enemy, and I hadn't even realized that I lost it. It sounds so stupid, but as this child in me was dying, it prompted me to come alive. In that moment, I realized the value of my life. Jesus paid a price for me and my life was designed to live for God and His glory. I hadn't yet had this revelation, but I knew something was changing, and it would be for the better. After the procedure was done, I felt empty. It felt like the aftermath of vomiting up everything you had eaten over the last few days. I was moved to the recovery room where I laid down trying to fall asleep, but couldn't, because all I could think about was that I was no longer having a baby. At that moment, I realized how adjusted I had become to the thought of being pregnant. I grew angry at myself. *Why did I go*

The Material Girl

through with it? Why did I do this? The emotions were so raw and out of control that I couldn't make out if I was sad, upset, pretending to care, or really caring. After about twenty minutes, a young lady came to my cot and asked me to drink some water and if I was okay to stand. I didn't physically feel bad. I was just an emotional wreck. I held it together and pretended that I was fine, until I saw him. I looked into the face of the guy who I blamed for this. If I would have had a gun, I could have killed him in that moment. I needed someone other than myself to blame and he was the easy target. So on the ride home, I remained quiet. His brother asked if I was okay, and I shook my head 'yes.' My dead child's father said nothing nor did he try to console me. He just acted like I came from a routine check-up with the doctor. However, nothing was normal—not the life I had become accustomed to, not him, not any of it.

By the time I made it back to my mom's house, the anger had festered long enough and erupted into an argument. I'm not sure how everything unraveled. All I can remember is that I called him all types of names, we started to argue, and he was gone. He left me there alone to soak in my own misery and figure it out by myself. I made some soup, ate, then laid on the couch, thinking to myself "what now?" I hoped the noise and pain would dissipate.

Reflection: Guiding Light

I want to help you do a self-evaluation. Although I am telling my story, I want every girl, boy, man, or woman reading this book to take something away from my experiences. I am not writing this to just spread all of my business on the streets, but instead to demonstrate who I was and the transformation to who I have become. Self-reflection is not easy, however it can be life changing and provide an opportunity for anyone to relearn themselves and fix the issues that may be causing us to have a harder life than God intended. The

What You Wear Can't Conceal Who You Are

Lord has been my guiding light through troubling times. Even when I didn't know it, I had people praying for me, pushing me closer to Him. These people didn't focus on what they saw, but instead they believed that I was already who God created me to be, versus the reflection I saw in the mirror. I encourage you to take just a moment to jot down situations in your life that have sculpted how you view things around you. At times, I have been caught in my social life and bound by others' perceptions of me. I've had issues with self-doubt, disbelief, and fear. You may not identify with all of these things, but there are undeniably moments, people, or feelings that have and are shaping you. You were created whole. God left nothing undone when He created you. Now it's time for you to tap into the things He has prepared for you and leave aside what you have prepared for yourself. Reflect in your journal on your guiding light. What thing has kept you moving and working towards have a better life. Use this time to appreciate the people and things around you that have kept you from losing your cool in the midst of a storm.

The Material Girl

Guiding Light

Chapter 3
Material Girl

Let's flashback to my first day of high school. This time period shaped the person I would evolve to be, the broken seventeen-year-old who had just aborted a baby. I was excited and full of energy. Prior to returning to school, my mom and grandmother took my sister, Nefertiti, and I to purchase clothes. I made it my purpose to only buy what was "in" that year. I selected as many Disney and Warner Bros (as we referred to them), shirts as my mother could afford. I went to the Gap and racked up on jeans and shorts, and we stopped by the outlets in Virginia at Potomac Mills, so I could get a few DKNY and Calvin Klein tees. Reebok and Adidas were the tennis shoes of the late 90s and I was determined to be hip. My hair had grown out from a disastrous butcher cut I had done to my hair, trying to remove braids two summers prior. I was and still am light-skin to the point where people assumed I was mixed, and I never had spats of acne or massive pimples. I did however have little chicklet teeth, and I had the nerve to have a chip slam in the middle of my mouth. My mom tried to force me to get braces in middle school, but since I was already dealing with being an ugly duckling, I refused. My mom took me to get my hair done the week before. My hair was a naturally beautiful sandy blonde, and I had

The Material Girl

natural highlights, that looked like hair color, during the summer. I even went to the nail salon to get a manicure, pedicure and arched eyebrows to prepare for my big day.

At the age of thirteen, when I entered high school, I felt like I was an adult and the decisions that I made from that point forward were based on what I wanted to do, not what my parents said. I can remember that first day of high school from almost eighteen-years-ago as clear as today. If my looks that morning were any indication of how well I would do in high school, I should have been a straight A student, but since they aren't, my story is a little different. August 1997, I woke up early in the morning to get myself ready. The summer went by so quickly, and I experienced a growth spurt like no other. I was previously 5'3 and weighed 160 pounds. I was not into black boys, because they weren't into me. I attracted Caucasians and Latinos, but by ninth grade, I was 130 pounds at 5'6, with nice thighs and a little butt. I fasted from chocolate the year before because I wanted so badly to have the Coca-Cola bottle shape that attracted the attention of boys my age. I knew nothing about a spiritual fast back then. That morning, my golden locks were freshly pressed in a wrap. My light skin was smooth and gleaming. I put on my Warner Bros shirt and my Gap jean shorts with a fresh new pair of black and white Samoa Adidas. I checked my hair in the mirror, applied my lip gloss, and went on my way. I got on the bus and was greeted by two of my close friends from middle school. We talked the whole way to school about who from middle school was going to our high school. We caught each other up on all of the summer gossip and compared class schedules. At that time, I was a French Immersion student; it was a program that I had been a part of since kindergarten, but I had been so caught up in the social aspect of school that I hadn't retained half of the knowledge I should have had by ninth grade. I exited the bus and joined my friends out

What You Wear Can't Conceal Who You Are

side of Central High School. We cracked a couple of jokes on each other, then I proceeded inside of the blue doors of my new school.

I had become a "material girl" with no pure substance, besides the things around me that I allowed to define me. So what life events brought me to that point? Well these stories will take some time to explain with many events that didn't seemed so life changing at the time. I didn't become the "material girl" overnight. It was a steady buildup of events. Looking back at my first day of high school, I could see how some of these habits began. I had bloomed into a beautiful flower, no longer getting talked about because of my size. As a defense mechanism, I developed a mouth that would make a grown man cry, so most of the time, I wasn't talked about to my face. If I was, the tongue lashing that person received was horrific. I don't think I was unlike the other kids my age. We were all going through natural transitions from kids to young adults, and we all had a little ugly in us.

When I first went to high school, I was caught up in the who's who. I attended school with one of my sisters, Harmony (on my father's side of the family; Harmony and I did not have the same mother, but we didn't grow up defining each other as half-sisters. We had a closer bond than me and Nefertiti, who lived in the same household as me) and since she was known as a fashionista, I felt I too had to live up to those same standards. I wish that as a teenager I was as strong-willed as I am now. If so, I would have been okay with being me, but I wasn't. I was caught up in being accepted and fitting in. It didn't help that my sister was rocking designer bags from Fendi, MCM, Gucci, all of it. Now my household wasn't built like that. My mom made decent money for her age and was, for the most part, raising me and my other sister, Nefertiti, on her own, financially anyway. I didn't have the luxury of spending hundreds of dollars on bags, shoes, or anything else. I'm not actually sure if

The Material Girl

my other sister's mom was buying these items for her or if they were coming from her own pocket, since she worked. Either way, I walked in the school doors and there was a standard that I was expected to uphold. I had no clue of the X that was on my back and how many people were looking to rip me apart.

    Now I had experienced this same scrutiny in middle school, but not as much as in high school. I had already overcome my ugly phase from middle school and was now this cute girl with shoulder-length golden hair who had the attention of older guys. However, I was kind of a tom boy who wore hush puppies, Adidas and of course my Reebok high tops, with baggy clothes from the Gap, Old Navy, Calvin Klein, DKNY, and Tommy Hilfiger. I tried my best to keep up with trends by begging my mom and grandma to take me to outlets so that I could find items at a discounted rate. I also wore my sisters' hand-me-down bags. I knew nothing about all of these top designers prior to entering high school, nor did I care about them. I just wanted to look pretty. Within a few months of my ninth grade year, I overheard people talking about me and encountered some conversations where I had to curse some people out for saying that I wasn't as fly as my sister. My sister was a fighter and she had a reputation of being pretty, fashionable, and young heavy weight. Back then, these traits would have been an equivalent of being a social media celebrity today. She was ninety-five pounds soaking wet, but could knock down someone twice her size. Me on the other hand, had fought before and could hold my own, but I was not interested in fighting girls or being caught up in drama. So I was faced with living up to the standards set by my petite sister, a Mike Tyson of our times, who had a killer shape and wore clothes that people twice her age couldn't afford. What was I supposed to do with that?

What You Wear Can't Conceal Who You Are

I, on the other hand, was this loud, giddy teenager, who loved looking good, joking, and being goofy with friends. I just enjoyed the social life of being in high school. My sister loved me and never once expected me to be like her. She LOVED and still does love fashion. It's a part of her make up, but I felt as if I had to adopt that same posture to avoid the criticism that came from the masses. It became crystal clear fairly quickly that I had to figure out a way to look, act, or be like my sister just to fit in. At that stage in my life, popularity seemed so vitally important to my existence, but oh how I was wrong. It felt like my future was hinged on the ability to stand out amongst the crowd because of how I looked. I don't know if I created that standard in my head, but at the time, I felt that it was created by the environment around me.

Overtime, I started working and had two jobs by the age of fifteen. I made a reasonable amount of money during that time. I was literally taking home between $500 to $600 every two weeks and spending it all on clothes, shoes, and hanging out with friends. If you show me your bank statement, I can tell you your values. Money is an indicator of people's values. If a person spends the majority of their earnings on investing, you can assume that they value investing and or preparing for retirement. My check book story then is totally different than what it is today. I was infatuated with looking good, partially because I was so self-conscious and at times felt ugly. Most people, even today, feel as though "things" make them important. Their things boost their self-confidence. That was me, and it wasn't until I became an adult that I learned to undo these misnomers that I had developed. The moments in high school that I felt forced to fit in and prove to everyone that I was as good as my sister was when I gave up my identity for someone else's. To this day, I look back and see some of those same people who I tried to impress struggling to still keep up with the Joneses with barely an education to provide for their families, working dead-end jobs,

The Material Girl

still living with their parents, but rocking Chanel, Louis, and Gucci, or even worse, homeless. The very same people that seemed to have it all worked out then are irrelevant to my life now. I don't say this to put anyone down, but instead to show how irrational my thinking was at the time. I was so obsessed with having things to impress people that I didn't like, who probably didn't like me, and are not here today.

Today I ask myself why we as a society place so much emphasis on the first day of school? How is a student's appearance or what they have on going to play a part in how successful they are in school? In my ten years as a high school teacher it never fails, every year students walk in the building excited and full of life, not because they are excited to learn, but because they are reunited with some friends and some enemies that they can show off their new outfits, kicks, and gadgets to. This of course proves how wealthy they are. Really? Most of the times these students' parents have robbed Peter to pay Paul, so they could go school shopping. Or, better yet, the students have worked all summer just to save up a few coins to go 'back to school' shopping. Is that what life has been minimized too: clothes, looks, and money—and nowadays, sex? The girl with the biggest butt or the nicest bag wins. I am so glad I have removed myself from that ideology, but the mere fact that I have to have so many conversations with young ladies regarding these things becomes saddening and frustrating, because there is so much more to life than things.

Days and years went by and I continued to set myself apart, or so I thought. I was a popular girl who knew all the upperclassmen and even dated a few. I knew everyone from my old middle school, and I had both enemies and 'frenemies', as well as my click. It's crazy how things in my life moved so fast. I am unsure how I went from a chatty sweet girl to a loud, boisterous, and at times, obnox-

What You Wear Can't Conceal Who You Are

ious chick that thought being socially seen was what high school and life was all about. I wore nice clothes, always had a fresh hairdo, and had a bad attitude. At that time, I loved to seem as though I had it all worked out on the exterior, but I truly felt empty inside playing charades of sorts. Overtime, I made it official with my first boyfriend and lost my virginity at the whopping age of fourteen, just three months before my fifteenth birthday and right before starting a summer job at Six Flags. On the outside, to a teenager, life was great. But on the inside it was a different story. For years, I masked and hid from the core of who I was and what I hated about me, which was ME. I really felt unintelligent, ugly, fat, or at times, too skinny, and unoccupied. I went through my teenage years fighting the very existence of who I was and often asked God why I was even born.

During my junior year of high school, I had a boyfriend who was four years my senior. We talk now about how he probably should have been arrested for dating me since I was only fifteen and he was nineteen-years-old. However, he wasn't necessarily a bad thing for me, although I had my bad girl ways, him being older, made me become more responsible and respectful to my parents and have a different outlook on life. He taught me how to drive, and he pushed me to be better in school. I realized how good I had it at home, since he was having personal issues with continually being put out of his mother's home. However, that relationship got boring fast and by the summer of my senior year, I was on to the next. My ex, Lamont, who could have become my "baby daddy" was an old high school crush. Ironically, I ran into him while my boyfriend at the time was waiting for me in the car. After we exchanged numbers, which was truly innocent at the time, he started calling and I started answering. His persistent calls and consistent interest made it clear that he wanted to become closer than just friends, and I was intrigued. When he was in the twelfth grade, I was in the tenth. He

The Material Girl

was the man back then. He had a car and was a star football player with girls all over him. But by the time we got together, he was out of high school. He had tried college for a year and then decided on trade school. So by the time we reconnected he was pursuing an IT certification. To me he was quite charming. He had been dating a stripper, which I should have known would be trouble, and he was one of those guys who everyone suspected was a hustler, but no one really knew. He wasn't flashy or arrogant, but somehow he always had money. I can't even remember if he actually had a legitimate job, but I didn't ask and he didn't tell. So as time progressed, I told my boyfriend at the time that it was over, and I embarked on a roller coaster ride with this newfound friendship. He had my attention my entire twelfth-grade year. He was my happiness, my best friend, my confidant, and he made me feel important. It's so funny how we look to others for security and to feel important when we really don't need another person on earth to validate our worth, because God already signed on that dotted line when he created us beautiful and unique. However, fast forwarding to ten months later: he still hadn't made me his girlfriend. Later, after all the drama, he joked and said that I was really his girlfriend, but he just refused to say it at that time. REALLY? We were doing grown up things. I was leaving school early for him to pick me up. We constantly fought over his ex and my insecurities. I swore he had someone else. Our once beautiful relationship had become a big ole mess. By the time I got pregnant, this guy who was once such a big deal had slowly fallen off of that pedestal and had become the scum of the earth.

My need to fit in, grow up fast, and be who everyone else said I should be, left me in a state of misery and confusion. I often wonder how my high school years would have ended if I had not fallen into the materialistic, fast girl trap. How many girls' lives would turn out differently if their high school years weren't spent chasing men, money, and attention? It's something to think about.

What You Wear Can't Conceal Who You Are

As an educator, I am compelled to reverse the fate for my girls. I know that life in high school seems to be so important and it's hard to see forward into the future and what really matters. But it's such a temporary time. It comes and goes, and the worst thing our young women and men can do is make decisions during high school that will negatively impact their lives forever.

Reflection: Purpose is Powerful

Living in a world that glorifies things it's hard not to admire and desire them. Nothing is wrong with wanting things; the issue with the desire for things is when it overshadows your drive and understanding of the importance of having good character and work habits to acquire the things in life you desire. When people start to kill over shoes or the claims to a block to sell drugs for monetary gain, we diminish the importance of life itself. When things or notoriety become more important than life itself it threatens to exterminate human's existence. That is when materialism has reached a point that harms our society.

My desire for things at that age didn't make me a bad person, but it created a person chasing after things instead of purpose. The initial desire to have nice clothes and shoes to be accepted, became the need for attention and affection, which turned into lust. It was a gradual addiction one hinging on the need for the other. Before I knew it, I had defined who I was and my worth based upon what I possessed. This notion that things produce value was dangerous because I no longer had an identity of my own—it was attached to things. I encourage you to do a self-evaluation of what you deem valuable. Go and look at your last month's bank statement or calendar to determine what do you spend your money and time on. These aspects of your life can uncover some hidden issues

The Material Girl

that may lay underneath your beautiful exterior. If you are spending most of your time on social media viewing what is going on in everyone else's life or running to the mall every time a new pair of Jordan's come out, you as a person no longer hold weight in your own life. You have given the power away to your environment, which tends to be deadly. You are now killing your purpose, your drive, and your self-identity, to conform to what everyone else is doing, saying, buying, and becoming.

After examining your life start planning and paying attention. Everyone has a desire to be wealthy but not everyone has the tenacity to create wealth. Make a commitment to yourself to wake up every day with a purpose. Whether it is save a hundred dollars or go to business seminars to get exposure to options out there. Or if it's just to build a stronger relationship with God, start working at it. Write down the things you spend most of your time on and then outline what it is you want to do to change the time you waste on things and create a plan. Nothing great has happened without a plan. Even if the plan starts out one way and ends in another, you at least had a goal set to accomplish. The more you plan, the more you will have clarity on what direction your life is headed. All it takes is one decision and actions.

What You Wear Can't Conceal Who You Are

Purpose is Powerful

The Material Girl

Chapter 4
My Material for His Material

Change didn't come immediately after enduring the abortion in March. For a short period of time I wanted to change. Having felt the residue of killing a blessing was traumatic, but life goes on, right? The months that followed were so compacted with events that I was able to distract myself from the pain. As I completed high school, I was extremely focused on finishing with decent grades so that I could attend Morgan State University. During this time, I was taking tests, completing financial aid applications, and packing for Morgan. I also had to make sure I had everything needed for prom and graduation and set aside time to hang out with friends and family before I left for school. By the time May came around, I was at the end of the road. I had finished high school and reached a milestone—I was entering adulthood. Despite things looking good on the outside, I didn't realize that I was carrying a weight on my shoulder that I couldn't and wouldn't discuss with anyone. As I mentioned, a couple of my friends knew about my secret, but the people who could have really helped me during this time had no clue.

The Material Girl

The year prior to the abortion in the summer of 2000, my aunt invited my mom, sister, and I to attend a church service at her church, Spirit of Faith Christian Center. My aunt wasn't a biological aunt. She was my older cousin who grew up with my mom, and they were close like sisters. She invited us casually, because the congregation had recently moved into a new building.

My mom encouraged us to attend, and I obliged, even though I had no real desire to wake up early on a Sunday to attend church. Despite how I felt, there was no way I would tell my mother "no." I still lived in her house, and at that point, she and I were on fairly good terms after getting through some of the headaches I caused her during my early teenage years.

Sunday morning arrived, and I woke up with no real expectations for that church service, however, God had other plans that day. He used my first time at Spirit of Faith to activate a desire in me that I still have today. We rode up to the building and to my surprise the church was in a strip mall. Not just any strip mall, but the one I can remember from my childhood. These buildings once housed liquor stores, convenient stores, and at a time, provided shelter for the homeless. I can recall riding past this very building to go to the club and didn't realize it had become a church. The building I saw before me on that Sunday was painted white with gold and purple accents, and big bright windows. They had a freshly painted parking lot, full of cars. I thought to myself, how big of a transformation that had been from the prior year. Seeing it that day was like God was showing me how he could turn something so fast from being dilapidated into something new. The inside was even more intriguing, not the typical church environment. There was no balcony or big cathedral ceilings, or pews for that matter. Just a bunch of upholstered purple chairs lined in rows from the front to the back of the sanctuary. I immediately felt comfortable. I could relate to

What You Wear Can't Conceal Who You Are

having a different outward appearance than what was really going on inside. Despite how much I wanted to act invisible, the energy in that atmosphere was magnetic. Church ladies and even young people my age came up to me and hugged me in the warmest way. The praise team sang and my heart jumped. Then, just as I was getting warmed up to the service thinking *this isn't so bad,* the pastor, Michael Freeman, stepped up to the pew and his words commanded my attention. That morning, I realized that I had a place in the kingdom of God and in that church body…

    I had never realized how much God loved me, despite me never really acknowledging Him in my life. I now know God has a specific assignment for my life, and no matter how many times I messed things up, He would always hold that position for me. Growing to this point of understanding His grace and goodness didn't happen instantly. It took quite some time, but once I grasped it, I knew that there is no greater feeling than the joy of the Lord being in my corner throughout my life's journey. Unbeknownst to me, God knew that I would need Him at that very moment—a pivotal time when I was at a crossroad between my past and my future—to push me through this extremely difficult time.

    Prior to attending this church service, I grew up visiting (I say "visiting" because we were never regulars) two churches, one Baptist and the other Presbyterian. All I knew about church was that I could lay in the pews to take a nap during service and expect refreshments, such as donuts and orange juice after it was over. When I attended the Baptist church with my grandmother, she made me attend Sunday school. I barely understood what they were talking about, but there were kids there and we could play and have fun. To me, church had not been important at all—it was more like recreation. It was cool when I went and cool if I didn't go. I never saw the purpose or meaning to fellowship. However, looking back, I

The Material Girl

find it intriguing how many parts of my life were influenced by people who believed in God and were "church-goers." However, their lifestyles never drew me close enough to want to attend church and meet God for myself. Since the age of nine, I had attended a dance studio that was based on Godly principles. The studio demonstrated its faith foundations in various ways. As dancers, we lifted our hands at the ends of performances, lifted our heads, and looked up to the sky to acknowledge God's presence. We danced to a slew of Kirk Franklin songs, quoted scriptures during practices, and learned biblical principles. Even still, this influence from the studio was not enough to keep me devoted to God. For a short period of time in ninth grade, I even went to church with one of my best friends and her family on the weekends. The church was huge and filled with people young and old, which is one of the reasons why I liked to attend. I was able to put on a cute outfit, strut through the halls as if I had a clue, and hear some good music. I actually could relate to some of the sermons the pastor would preach, so for me, that was a Sunday well spent. The deficit in all of these situations was that I still went home empty. I could not retain or apply any of the teachings I'd heard. I was still searching to find all the answers for myself. In hindsight, I know that despite what I did or did not retain, God used those situations to place seeds in me that would eventually grow so that He could use my life for this very purpose—to reach others.

Reflection: God's Nuggets

I want to pause right here. Thus far, reflections have been at the ends of chapters, but I believe this is a good point to stop and think. How has God used other people's influence and exposure, or even experiences, to draw you close to Him? God is such a loving God that He has thought about you well before you were even born.

What You Wear Can't Conceal Who You Are

So much so that even if you were born in the most horrific situation, He has strategically dropped nuggets and seeds along the way to pull you closer and draw you near Him. It's not by happenstance that your best friend's mother is a preacher or that your co-worker, who you really like keeps inviting you to his/her church, or that your high school is located right next to a church and you walk past it every day to and from school. Look at your life and you will see the goodness of God around you. Most of us tend to focus on what is blatantly in front of us or what is apparent and obvious, however, if you look deeper into your upbringing and surrounding, you will find God somewhere (and if you look close enough, everywhere). Take the time to find the connections or peace within that demonstrates His love for you.

Many of us get ourselves into situations that we would never be able to escape alone. However, so often, we diminish God's significance in our lives because we imagine that He can't care because we did *this* or we behave like *that*. God does care. He sees past our flaws and only sees the people He created us to be. Imagine that one person on the sidelines cheering for you that you have never met, but they simply see your ability to succeed. That's how God is. His love is not determined by our circumstances in life but only by His grace that He bestows on us—His sons and daughters.

Before moving past this point, right down everything you feel like you have done that prevents you from experiencing a good life. Then next to that list, write, "But God LOVES me!" By the end of this book, you will be able to see how much He loves you. My reflections are designed to essentially help you understand how God works and is moving in your life. Believe in His words. Build a relationship with your spirit being, and love yourself. No matter what you have done, God has you in mind and even when you don't feel like it, pull out that list, add that thing you did, and at the end write, "BUT GOD LOVES ME!"

The Material Girl

God's Nuggets

A New Direction

Okay back to my story. That morning when I arose to attend Spirit of Faith Christian Center with my mom, I had no second thoughts about what I would experience. I just knew there would be people. I loved gospel music, especially Kirk Franklin, and I was excited for my chance to dress up and look fly. All of these components together equaled a win for me. However, attending this church was nothing like I had ever experienced before. People welcomed me at the door; people who we didn't know began to hug us, and members of the church at every contact consistently showed us love. The service came to a point where they asked for visitors to stand up to be acknowledged. At that time, I was so nervous because I knew that all eyes would be on me in the house of the Lord. I felt like I was in a room full of people with no clothes on and everybody was pointing and staring at me (you know how that dreadful illustration goes—the one that makes everyone feel REALLY uncomfortable). I stood up despite my initial feelings of fear, and I was greeted with handshakes and hugs, as well as a "thank you for attending" gift. I spent the remainder of the service observing everyone's actions. They stood and lifted their hands when the music played. When the pastor stood up, the congregation saluted him as if he were some kind of military sergeant. Within an hour into the service, the pastor began to preach, and I spent most of my time searching through the bible trying to find the scriptures he named.

The Material Girl

I wish I could tell you that a profound word was given that drew me in, but truth is I can't even remember what the sermon was about that day. Nonetheless, somehow there was a connection made for me that day. I could understand some of the principals the pastor discussed and I didn't feel like he spoke a bunch of hocus pocus about spirituality. Although it was hard for me to keep up with everything, an emotion erupted and triggered something in me to want to find out more. Looking back, I know it was God. That one encounter created a desire in me that I had no clue would change my life forever.

After two hours of the singing, church announcements, dancing, and teaching from the pastor, the end of the service was near. The pastor started to give an appeal. The entire church was instructed to close their eyes and we were reassured that no one would see the individual responses to questions that would follow. The pastor went on to ask us four important questions:

1. If you died today are you certain your name would be found in the Lamb's book of life? (Me: "Ummmm I don't think so, and what is that?")

2. Do you need to repent for your sins and rededicate your life to God? (Me: "What is repent? I have plenty of sins, but I never dedicated my life to Him in the first place?")

3. Was I filled with the Spirit with the evidence of speaking with tongues? (Me: What tongues? I have a tongue!"); and

4. Do you want to join the church? (Me: "Okay! That sounds cool!").

So, while my eyes were closed, I wanted so badly to understand these questions, so I raised my hands, but at the same time, I wondered if my mom and sister felt the same pull I did to raise their hands for the appeals. I was so scared to die and not know where I would go. And even if this place called heaven didn't exist, I reasoned, I'd rather take the chance of believing than risk the chance of not believing and miss my chance at heaven. Once "the appeal" was over, those who raised our hands were asked to stand and go to the front. Unlike before when asked to stand as a visitor, I jumped up. When I reflect on that moment, I think of how strategic the process was; I had no time to consider my surroundings. I could only rely on my ears to gauge my understanding of information so that my heart could be open to new possibilities. At that point, I was ready to learn more about this God that the preacher spoke about and how He would help me figure out my purpose on earth. My sister and I walked to the alter and confessed our belief in God and His son Jesus.

Prior to attending this church, I knew that I wanted to be a better person and that God exists. But I had no clue how strong His presence was throughout my life until I accepted Him and started to see Him as Lord and Savior of my life. At that moment, God was able to reveal Himself in me. I can remember as a youngster growing up, I would close my eyes from time-to-time and just imagine what the world would be like if nothing had existed. I had no clue why I was doing this or what my purpose was, but I was always curious about what life was like before all the mayhem. Noise and life distractions had occupied my life, and I yearned for more—what if none of these things had never happened? What was my life like before it all? I knew that God put me here for something but I had no clue what that something was. I just wanted to know where I came from and how I just mysteriously ended up in this earth. I can remember the first time I read Genesis chapter one; my behavior during my younger years made so much sense to me. Genesis 1:1-5 reads, "In the beginning God created the heavens and the earth. The earth was without form, and void; and darkness was[a] on the face of the deep. And the Spirit of God was hovering over the face of the waters. Then God said, "Let there be light"; and there was light. And God saw the light, that it was good; and God divided the light from the darkness. God called the light Day, and the darkness He called Night. So the evening and the morning were the first day."

At sixteen, my life was full of darkness, void of form or spiritual knowledge, and I so badly wanted to be light. That summer day, I accepted Jesus Christ as Lord of my life in hopes that His light could shine through me. I have this understanding today as I write this book, but back then, I didn't. Unfortunately, the high I felt after first being saved lasted merely a second, and after that, life went on as usual.

I went back to attend the church a few times with my mom throughout the year, and every time I returned, I can recall wanting to know more. So by the time I was seventeen and my senior year was coming to an end, I started to attend the church more and more. I had my license and was able to go on my own because my mom sometimes didn't feel like attending. After I got pregnant and had the abortion, I really didn't miss a Sunday at church leading up to leaving for college. Three months later, it was June. My high school sweetheart (and the guy that I gave my virginity to) Roger had reappeared, and he was a good distraction from the pain I had experienced. He and I had been dating on and off since I was fourteen. Roger was the complete opposite from Lamont. He didn't have much money; he wasn't flashy or arrogant, just a sweet guy who really cared for me. That's not to say he didn't have his issues, since the main reason we weren't together was because he couldn't remain faithful and loyal to me. Every time I broke up with another guy, he was right there waiting to mend what we had back together. We attended my prom together and I felt happy again. Soon after that, I graduated high school and prepared to embark on college.

What You Wear Can't Conceal Who You Are

As I was walking into those college days, however, I had the weight of the world on me. I could not describe it and there was no one I could share this with so I buried it deep within my heart. I made the decision not to discuss the events of the prior school year ever again. Even when I hooked back up with Roger, I believe it was only to prove to myself that I was ready to move on. However, over time that relationship started to present an entirely new set of problems for me, which I'll discuss in a later chapter. By June of that same year, I was silent. I didn't talk about the events from March with anyone, not with my friends and not even with my ex. I couldn't even discuss it with myself. I simply acted as if nothing ever happened, which was the worst remedy for my sickness.

Eventually, school started and I found myself going to church quite frequently when I came home for the weekend. I'm not sure if it was that invisible weight that piqued my curiosity or the fact that I was looking for answers and every time I heard a word from the pastor it resonated in my soul. It was as if his words were invisible strings pulling me closer to the answers I needed for my life. I know that although I was functioning in society, I was in a dire state of depression and my emotional state was very unstable. My body and heart were numb to feeling the compassion I once felt for people around me, and I was out for blood. I felt like I wasn't loved or cared for so I went through life doing and saying whatever made me feel good at the time. When I connected with Spirit of Faith, I felt human again. However, that moment of serenity didn't stop the turmoil I felt throughout my week. So when I was away at school, I partied my sorrow away. I may not have been intoxicated every day of the week, but I drank and partied enough to subdue my emotions.

With no hope in my heart, I entered into those holy doors on Sundays. I was terrified of the judgment that God would give

The Material Girl

me since I knew what I was doing and what I had done. It was sin. But what could outweigh killing an unborn child? I had committed the ultimate sin, or so I thought. Because of this, I thought, *so what if I add partying to my list of bad deeds? Nothing is worse than what I've done.* I was young, and I had no clue and no understanding of the true revelation of God's word. Back then, all I could think was that once people found out, I would be cast off and no one would really trust me or allow me to have a good life. In short, I felt condemned. I had not yet been introduced to the word, and that there is no condemnation for those who are in Christ Jesus (Romans 8:1).

So I went to church every Sunday and stayed neutral, trying to blend into the background and just hear the word and go back to my regularly scheduled program. I heard lessons about God's grace and love for me; this gave me comfort and made me come back. I also genuinely wanted to change my life and I learned that I could cast my sins into the depth of the sea and be forgiven. I was clueless, but my lack of knowledge and ignorance was my best defense and gave me the ability to be open and search for answers.

The time I spent at church kept me from losing my mind and turning to the world for answers. I have learned that everyone has their breaking point and that the day I had an abortion was mine. For some, my breaking point may seem so minuscule. However, for me—a person who always wanted children—killing a seed that would resemble, act, and grow to call me "mom" was devastating. Even today, as a thirty-three-year old woman, I am writing a book about my struggles and still face them every day. I am single, with no husband, no potential suiter, and no children. However, I have mothered many and help groom hundreds of young ladies, but have birthed none. At times, I feel like that desire will never be fulfilled because of my past decisions. God is the answer, but He is not always the solution to a problem. Most of the time we are our own problem standing in the way. So often we want to reap what we have not sown, we want the glitz and glamour, but never work hard to obtain it, or don't want to change. It is human nature to want to live and act the way our natural minds see fit. This dynamic is so hard to comprehend and is why faith is so important. Believing a spirit being that we can't necessarily see with our natural eyes or touch is hard for a lot of people. We have choices to make in life and as long as we do it without God or Holy Spirit, we will end up in bad situations that cost us. Each day, I acknowledge the power of fear and doubt, but I also counteract it with the power of God's love and grace. This is to remind myself that even when I feel inadequate, He is adequate. Even when I feel unloved, He is love. Even when I am friendless, He is my friend. By the time I was eighteen, I made a decision to attend church every time I came home. I wanted to work on fixing what was broken within myself. This was not an easy task, but I was committed because I found joy and solace in God's word.

Overtime and with every new revelation, I began bartering my habit for his habit and my way for his ways. I still loved to be the center of attention, but found it less attractive than before. A shift had occurred. The shift was so subtle that I myself almost didn't see it. However, the people around me did and didn't let me forget it. My so-called friends would remind me that I was just drinking and partying a few days prior, and they questioned how I could be changed. It's rather funny how when people make a decision to do good we have to leave some "friends" behind. It didn't help that I was walking in unchartered territory. Feeling alone while doing it made things much harder. This process by no means was easy or happened quickly. It was a slow and steady race. It started with me making a decision and sticking to it. However, I found that on my way, God meticulously set people in my life to push me as He pulled me through hard times.

The Material Girl

Attending a church that taught me how to search for answers and knowledge was the start, but my *own* actions—applying the answers I found to my real life situations—was what transformed me. It wasn't until my junior year of college that I really started to change. First, the cursing stopped. I knew that my mouth was bad when one of my friends pointed out how much I cursed unnecessarily. She couldn't understand why I felt the need to use a curse word as if that helped me get my point across even more. Well it didn't! After she told me that, I started to feel like I was trying too hard to meet some criteria. It was as if there were some imaginary word count and contest on how much vulgar language I could use in one sentence. That year, I made a decision to stop cursing. Now realize I had made that same declaration a year before with no success, but by this time, I had been attending church for two years consistently. I was learning more about how God works. I admired people who I met from the church who were able to refrain from sex or drinking or cursing, because I *just* wasn't there yet. I was saved and learning His ways as well as learning how to love myself as He loves me. But I wasn't willing to give up the things that made me feel important and relevant, just not yet. I had built up will power and strength to do things differently. My desire to hang out at clubs and drink had diminished and the desire to live life righteously had increased.

I recently watched a teaching broadcast of a well-known young teacher in North Carolina who taught a lesson entitled "The Pull." This lesson was grounded in the very principle I'm sharing with you that most people don't get. God will put people in our lives that push us closer to Him, however, He is always the force pulling us to higher heights. I found the illustration he chose to use to demonstrate this intriguing. He took a bow and arrow and tried to push the arrow to go somewhere. Now we all know that arrows won't go that far if you place them in the bow and push it because the bow was never designed for that purpose. The elastic band on the bow was meant to be pulled which uses a greater amount of strength to propel the arrow to a further distance. A person who practices archery must find the right force to hit the center of the bullseye. The factors that contribute to this success have a lot to do with practice, understanding the elements around that contribute to the trajectory, and aim. God is the archer and we are His arrows who, if we let Him, can propel us in the right direction to hit the mark. However, so often, we try to be the archer and the arrow, which, might I add, is impossible, and this causes us to miss every time.

    I made a small decision to stop cursing which was the first step in allowing God to be my archer and I didn't even know it. I had no clue how I would really stop cursing, because it was just a part of who I had become, but by simply allowing Him to guide me, it happened so easily that it felt like I stopped cursing overnight. I can even recall a guy at my college asking me had I stopped cursing. He was someone that was often around during social events, but he wasn't a close friend. When he asked me that question I was confused. He later revealed that he noticed how I substitute my foul language for other words and he wanted to do the same. That one moment for me was paramount because I didn't even realize how my one act of obedience had motivated someone else to change.

    The changes to my life happened continually like this one. Little by little, I made decisions to carry my life differently. I even became increasingly uncomfortable in certain places and around certain people. It wasn't because they were horrible, but God was working on something with me. His pull was greater than mine, and He was winning at the tug-of-war game I had played in years' past. To this day, I have some challenges in areas of my life, but I continually find power in His word, prayer, and my love for Him. I

The Material Girl

grew and started to love Him so much that I cared about nothing else but pleasing Him—not others. Even at times, I will care less about what my mom has to say about things (anyone who knows me knows she is my most favorite person on this earth), but I will choose God over anybody at this point in my life. I find it disappointing when I miss a mark or fall short. My journey of replacing my things for His things is never over. I always find that God is pulling me to grow more and more in different areas. So by no means have I arrived or am I perfect, but I'm perfectly perfecting the things that concern Him each and every day. I am consistently seeking the happiness, peace, and my full potential, which can only be realized through intimacy with God. Soon I was moving far away from that material girl I had come to know and closer to becoming His girl, clothed in glory and righteousness. Later in this book, in chapters nine, ten, and eleven, I will share strategies to help you make these changes in your life. My story may not look like yours, but you can still take some of what I've learned to help yourself.

Reflection: The Pull

People that see me like to think that I am perfect! Phahahaha…….. I could go down the list of things I have done and how imperfect I am. However, everyone makes their own assumptions based on their experiences or personal doubt that makes them believe they cannot accomplish what I have. I would have never thought in a million plus years that I would be an author—not only an author, but a teacher, and business owner. I always saw myself in business, but NEVER in this capacity. Instead of trying to write my own story, I allowed God to guide me. I have relinquished the responsibility to Him to give me a better life. My way wasn't working, and I found it easier to watch Him work. At times, I question Him, because my vision is not as clear as His, so I TRUST HIM!

What You Wear Can't Conceal Who You Are

Trusting God is the most important ingredient to growth and having a good life. It is fascinating to me now that people will trust the government with their taxes, the bank with their money, and even their significant others to provide them with security, love, and their livelihood, but will question God. The One who knows EVERYTHING, who is omnipresent (everywhere at the same time), and who can make a way out of no way, does not have our trust. People are scared to follow Him. I got tired of running the race with a bunch of people, but still feeling alone. It wasn't until I started to follow the one who could truly lead me did I see a shift in my life.

I call this the pull not the push! I mentioned that God is the One pulling you and He will send people to push you to help guide you to the destination He has set up for you. Instead of you pushing and pulling yourself in all these multitude of directions, which get you nowhere, look at letting go of the tug-of-war rope and watch God do His work. In this part of the book, I want you to jot down all of your bad habits—from your dirty car to drinking and clubbing. NOW be honest. You are the only one who will see this, so be completely transparent with yourself about where you are. This list will become your pull list. These are the things God is pulling you from. He is removing them from your life because they serve you no good purpose. It's important not to discredit anything on this list. Something as small as a junky room can be significant to what He wants you to change so that He can give you more. Throughout my journey, I've learned that even the small things on our minds that we need to get in order are not insignificant. Pay attention to those things, because they could be the one thing that helps or hinders you from entering into that next big opportunity.

The Material Girl

Write your "Pull List" here…………

Chapter 5
I Serve Multiple Masters

After high school, I dove head first into college by first attending pre-college from June to August to prepare myself for the change in atmosphere and new responsibilities college would bring. I left for college optimistic about what the future held. After prom, I rekindled my relationship with my first "love" Roger. I attended church regularly, and I was learning new things about myself every day.

For a long time, I couldn't quite understand why I had to work ten times harder than most to remain focused and complete my assignments. So at a young age, I labeled myself as the "dumb kid." Enrolling in college and doing fairly well in pre-college helped boost my self-confidence. I believed in myself, that I could do much better in college than I had in high school. This meant that I had to prioritize studying, practicing, doing homework, and putting forth an effort to learn over socializing. This worked for a little while, until I got sucked into the social life and freedom.

Roger and I barely made it an entire month in our relationship until the whirlwind of drama started; I was not interested in entertaining it either. In between the two years of us being sepa-

The Material Girl

rated, he had been back with his ex-girlfriend. Unbeknownst to me, she had a baby girl the year prior to us rekindling our relationship. He made it clear that the little girl was not his, and in fact, he was away at school when she was born. Soon, this story changed within the first month of our relationship. While he was away, his family started to tell him that his ex's baby looked just like him. So once he came home and actually saw the baby, he too believed that she could be his child. After further investigation, and a paternity test, he learned that this beautiful little girl was indeed his daughter.

This situation was just too close to home for me. I was still dealing with terminating a pregnancy, to then be faced with trying to support an eighteen-year-old boyfriend who became a father overnight. Being around his daughter brought me so much joy and I couldn't help but to feel guilty. I opened my heart up to this baby, which was not mine, but I had closed my heart to my own seed—and was still trying to forget the decision that I had made. This, coupled with a host of other emotions, including my desire to explore my adulthood and singleness in college, led us to breaking up. I decided to break up with Roger during the first month into the Fall semester of my freshman year. I was still trying to figure things out and adding a relationship to the situation wasn't helping.

That semester, I officially started my freshman year at Morgan completely embracing my freedom and independence, but before I knew it, I was back in another relationship by the middle of my freshman year. Of course that relationship lasted all of five minutes, and by the end of February of the Spring semester, I had called it quits. Throughout all of these short-lived on-again-off-again relationships, I never thought anything was wrong. I didn't see these flings as indication of my inability to be alone. However, now as a woman in my thirties, it is clear that I was looking for acceptance in so many different areas of my life. In my mind, I was just having fun. I was young and wasn't looking to marry any of these guys. The momentary relationships provided me with the security that I so desperately needed at the time. Even writing this chapter brings about so much shame and regret. I still feel like an idiot sometimes, knowing that I spent so much time trying to get other people to accept me, especially men. I wasted time and lowered my standards to only end up in the same place I was prior to meeting them. My less-than-tactical approach to dating and relationships caused me multiple heart breaks and disappointments time after time. Some of these heartbreaks actually left me emotionally unstable. It hurt to only have these guys' approval for a short period of time until they found something else or someone more attractive to chase. I made so many excuses like, "It's them, not me," but after a while, you start to really think it is you, no matter how great you are.

    I have found that some of the most successful people are still some of the loneliest, because they have not realized their self-worth. Therefore, nothing anybody can give them or do for them will sustain the missing pieces to their own puzzles, which is God. What seems so simple isn't always so practical. As a young adult, God doesn't seem fun or enlightening. You want to enjoy life without any restrictions on where you can go or what you can do. Back then, getting saved didn't change my desire to live young and free. However, it did hold me accountable to a lifestyle that I never knew existed. My primary examples of "the good life" were portrayed on TV, in movies, or through music. Although I was going to church on the weekends and learning so much, I was still confused as to how to live a fulfilling life. I was playing double-dutch with my life and it would soon catch up to me. I often tell people that you can't serve multiple masters and expect both to give you what you want. I was working full time trying to maintain the appearance that I was doing great, while partially toying with the idea of living a Godly lifestyle.

The Material Girl

Constantly playing tug-of-war becomes draining. I was tittering between the old me and discovering who God called me to be. Most people want the good life, but don't want to work hard to get it.

The unhealthy relationship choices were just a few of the problems I had. I partied all throughout the week, maxed out credit cards spending money I didn't have, and had multiple overdraft fees that I tried to hide from my mom. After my freshman year, I refused to live on campus, so I worked the entire summer to save up for a car and a down payment for an apartment. I had no choice but to work while in college, because if I wanted to keep up the appearance of things, I needed money. This is not to say I wasn't a hard worker, but had I not been so focused on having "things," I could have really appreciated that season in my life. I could have spent more time networking, preparing for life after college, or simply reflecting.

Now don't get me wrong, college wasn't completely a disaster. By my junior year, I had started to figure things out and was maintaining a 3.0 GPA. I had a steady job at the bank and was involved with student government, as well as a host of other organizations on campus. I stopped all the partying and focused more on my relationship with God; it came with sacrificing some relationships, but gaining others. The one factor that helped me change was being consistent. I went to church and read my bible for clarity and understanding. Although things didn't change overnight for me, my faithfulness, time, and determination to never return to that dark place, made such a difference in my life. The saying "ignorance is bliss," is so accurate, because when you are unaware it makes it easier to do things without a conscious or as I like to say, without Holy Spirit beating you up. On the flip side, the knowledge I obtained from church and my reading created the tenacity I would need to sustain me through troubled times and keep me on a path to uncovering my purpose. In the game of tug-of-war, someone has to win.

It is usually the one who has prepared for the war, the one who has more power and strength. So as strong willed as I may have thought I was, God's word was stronger.

Matthew 6:22-24 (TLB) states, *If your eye is pure, there will be sunshine in your soul. But if your eye is clouded with evil thoughts and desires, you are in deep spiritual darkness. And oh, how deep that darkness can be! You cannot serve two masters: God and money. For you will hate one and love the other, or else the other way around.*

This one scripture explains my life in its entirety at that time. I made a decision to dwell in light by seeking out his presence on a consistent basis. Every Sunday that I sat in that church building, the word ate away a dark piece of me. This process remains even today. I die to parts of myself that don't work well with my purpose. Although I was never strung out on drugs nor did I face what some people may see as an "obstacle," for me, learning how to love myself was crucial in my growth process. Without self-love we can never be who God designed us to be, because we will not believe in ourselves and God's ability to transform us into His masterpieces. More than ever, I learned that nothing happens overnight. In a world filled with a false sense of success or as many call it a "popcorn society" or "microwave culture," understanding that God's process takes time helped build my faith.

Reflection: Die Daily

In the previous chapter, you created a "Pull List," and wrote down the behaviors that God is pulling you from. Here, with your

"Pull List" in mind, I would like you to identify daily habits that you could implement that will enable you to die to your flesh. What will you stop doing daily? How can you surrender your self-gratifying desires to God so that He can transform you? Remember how I mentioned that the first change that I noticed in myself was that I stopped cursing? In order to do this, I had to first acknowledge that I had a problem, then figure out a way I could make adjustments to that problem. For me it was replacing those words with other words that meant the same thing. For a while I wouldn't say the curse word; I would say the first letter, which sounds so stupid when saying it that eventually makes you stop saying it all together. I would say things like, "F him!" I was lucky to have people around me to tell me how stupid this sounded. My friends and others would be so confused as to why I didn't say the entire word and would say things like, "You might as well say the word because your intent on cursing is still obvious." After hearing these types of statements over and over again, the desire to say even the letter was gone. I not only had people around me who were honest but who also held me accountable to the goals I set for myself. Accountability is important.

When making changes in your life, you need people who want the same things you want in life and are able to help you stay focused on those things. Although I had lost some friends, I gained others and I started to surround myself with people who were chasing after the same clarity I was from God. By implementing those simple techniques, my speech was transformed and other bad habits, behaviors, and beliefs followed. For each item on your pull list, create another list of replacement behaviors. Things you can do to replace the negative behaviors. So, if you have regularly been late to work, your replacement could be getting to work thirty minutes early. This may not happen right away, but pushing yourself to get there thirty minutes before you are supposed to will help you reor-

What You Wear Can't Conceal Who You Are

ganize your time if now your goal is to arrive at 8 a.m. versus 8:30 a.m. Then tell a friend that will hold you accountable to your new desired behaviors. Not saying this person has to be perfect and have it all figured out, but they love you enough to tell you when you are falling off. It also must be a person you respect and one whose opinion you honor. If you are incorporating these things in your life you will begin to see the changes to your behavior and before you know it, these bad habits will no longer exist.

The Material Girl

Reflection: Fix It

Chapter 6
The Root

It was Thanksgiving of 2013, and I was back with my ex Kevin, who had just been released from jail (for the second time during our off and on relationship) three weeks prior. For some reason, I thought things could work, despite our rocky history... Kevin and I had known each other since 2001. I was seventeen when we met, and he was actually the cousin of one of my childhood friends. We never dated initially although he tried. At the time, I was dealing with my breakup with Roger and was starting college. Within a few months of us talking, he was arrested and went on trial. We kept in touch over the year and I actually went to visit him in jail prior to him being sentenced. Kevin was tried and convicted of attempted murder and sentenced to eight years in a federal prison. So when my friend told me how long he would be in prison, I had no real intentions on pursuing him at all. Even prior to his arrest, I felt like he wasn't my type. He was a hard core thug and seemed so rough, and I wasn't use to that. Although Lamont was a so-called "hustler," he wasn't in the hood or really a street dude. Kevin however, was nothing but HOOD! He grew up in one of the roughest parts of D.C. and had been exposed to drugs at an early age. I, myself, was born

The Material Girl

in the city, but I wasn't raised by the streets nor was I exposed to that life. As soon as my mother could afford it, she moved my sister and I to the suburbs in Maryland.

Kevin kept in touch with me while I was in college. Every time I changed my phone number he asked a friend of mine for it, and he would call me collect from jail. I answered his calls and talked with him, because I figured he needed some conversation and support while he was in prison. However, he had other intentions that I had no clue about at the time. He saw me as a good girl, one in school, making something of herself, who had her head on straight. He wanted me to be the Bonnie to his Clyde all while being a top executive in a major Fortune 500 corporation. It was as if he had this picture of me being some type of savior with the ability to help him get out of his situation and on the right path. Down deep I really think he wanted me to be able to change identities and put on a mask like some superhero. By day I was this working woman with a distinguished career, and at night I was making moves for my hustler boyfriend. In his mind I had things so well figured out that I could juggle both worlds. Unfortunately, his perception of me couldn't have been further from the truth. I was barely staying afloat, and I often felt like I was drowning in my own feces. So as time went on, I forgot about him, but he didn't forget about me.

In 2007, I started to hear from him more frequently. By this time, I was a teacher and working to earn my certification. He would call once a month or every other month and we would hold very intellectual conversations. He asked me about my day and my career and we would also talk about the bible. He was raised in a Christian household and had been reading the bible and other books in prison. He would tell me of all the different books he had read and would enlighten me on things I had never heard of before. Overtime, these casual conversations grew more intimate. He was always respectable and never overly aggressive. We started to write each other and I became a pen pal to him. He told me that he liked me, but he wanted to keep a distance between us, because he knew that I was focused. I was starting to grow feelings for him, and I shared this with him. To me it just seemed like he needed someone whom he could trust and who was outside of his world. He wanted better for himself, and at the time, I thought I could help him. His hardness coupled with his intellect was intriguing to me. He was far from your typical street dude and had a great spirit, even though he was living in hell. By 2008, we built a friendship that I enjoyed.

For a few months, I didn't hear from him, which was odd, but I continued life as usual. Still, I was in and out of relationships, dealing with this guy and that guy. By September of that year, I received a call from my friend. She told me that someone wanted to talk to me, and to my surprise, Kevin's voice came through the phone. At the time, I had no clue who he was and couldn't make out his voice. He got so annoyed by me that he gave her back the phone and we didn't talk after that for months.

Months later, I was leaving a Wednesday night bible study, and an unknown number scrolled across my screen. Not sure who it was, I answered anyway, and it was Kevin. We started talking and picked up where we had left off months prior. At that time, my friend had already told me he was back with his ex and living with her. This didn't bother me that much because I had no plans on being in a relationship with him or taking him serious at all. I just had an innocent crush and entertained him from time-to-time. He served a little over six years of his eight-year sentence and had a lot of adjusting to do.

By that November, Kevin and I were inseparable. He was still living with the girlfriend but spending all his time with me. She started to figure things out and knew his attention was going else where. So he moved out of her place and crashed on my friend's couch. This gave me easier access to him since she lived down the street from me and solidified our relationship even more. We talked all the time and found ways to hang out almost every day, even with me working in Baltimore and him living in D.C. Prior to getting with him, I had been practicing abstinence for almost two years and had stuck to it well. I even held out for quite some time with him, until I was tired of just patting and feeling. For a while, it was cool. We hung out when I wasn't at work, and some nights, he stayed at my place. This changed quickly. We had decided to make it official, but we had one problem: I enjoyed having multiple male (platonic) friends. One day we had a disagreement about having friends outside of our relationship. I felt like there was nothing wrong with entertaining other guys just as long as I kept it neutral and platonic. He, on the other hand, felt like we were all each other needed. I was only twenty-four; we weren't engaged, so I felt he was being controlling by telling me that I couldn't talk to other men. Although I never intended to do anything with them, I just didn't want anyone—not even my boyfriend—to have a say over who I did or didn't have in my life. Kevin was pissed. He didn't like the idea and figured his best way to get back at me was to show me how dangerous friends were.

 By the summer of 2009, our relationship was in shambles. I was living a double life. I enrolled in the Spirit of Faith Bible Institute to learn more about the word, but at night, I was fornicating or arguing with my man. He was getting late-night phone calls, leaving at all hours and staying out late in the clubs. We were constantly at each other's throats. Eventually, we broke up, and within months of us being apart, he was in trouble with the law again. Even though we weren't in the greatest place, when he was arrested, I stuck by him through the process. Kevin was eventually sentenced to thirty-six months in prison, and I was shook. I didn't know how to be a so-called "ride or die chick." I wasn't groomed for that lifestyle. That epiphany hit me when I went to Florida to visit him while he was in prison. The time we spent together was cool, but to see how he had to live was horrifying. On the last day of my visit, I cried. I knew I would not be back again to see him, because it hurt too bad. I felt like I had to choose: it was this life or God's life. In my head, I kept hearing Holy Spirit asking me, "Is this the good life?" Not to mention, I wanted attention from a man that he could no longer provide. I never really got rid of my "friends," and when we started battling, I had developed a new interest.

 I broke things off with Kevin as soon as I got back home from my visit, but that wasn't the end of it. When he came home in 2012, we started up again. Initially I was standoffish, but then I fell for him all over again. He was so charming and seemed so sincere, until he felt like I did something to hurt him. He had an "I will get you before you get me" mentality and a bad temper.

 Things were good for a while until Thanksgiving of 2013. Around this time, he found text messages in my phone between me and another guy. I wasn't cheating on him, but I was entertaining conversations with other men. Well this day in particular things turned really bad real fast. We went from me trying to explain the conversation to us physically fighting in his car, while his cousin was driving. I was kicking, swinging, and screaming while he had his hands clasped around my neck. I don't even think he realized what he was doing, but the look in his eyes was evil. He didn't see me as a woman he loved, but as his enemy. Granted, I did take the first swing, but his inability to control himself scared me. This was a mess, I told my sisters about this ordeal and they were furious. They called a "sister intervention" to try to get me to tell my dad, but I was so scared of what he may do or how he would look at me for being in this situation, so I refused. This caused so much friction between my sisters and I. Approaching the big thirty, with my birthday in four days, I felt like my life in four short months had fallen back to pieces. The bones of my past had resurfaced, and all I wanted to do was bury them again.

Even after this ordeal when everyone told me to walk away, I still tried to work things out with Kevin. He gave me the cold shoulder. Despite being rejected publicly, behind closed doors, when my friends weren't around, I tried to win him back. Not too long after this, my world changed and my eyes were opened. I knew he was dealing with someone(s) else, but I was in denial about how far he would take it with these other women.

While I was working on a job application for him, he trusted me with the password to his email account. One day, I logged in; I wasn't snooping, just trying to find an email from a job application I filled out for him. Somehow, something so innocent led to me trying to find a way to see his pictures. At first there was nothing alarming. But once I was able to uncover everything, it all came to a head. I saw videos of him with other women and nude pictures of another woman. I was humiliated. I wanted him to love me and only me. To learn that he could have sex with all these women *and lie to me* was unbearable. When I confronted him about it, he completely turned on me. *Apparently,* it was my fault!

After this relationship, I went into a major depression. I did not want to talk to anybody or do anything. My outlet was partying. I did not open my bible. I did not talk to my friends, and I barely went to church. I felt like my esteem was with him, and when he left me, he took it with him. It got so bad that in the mist of one of my rants, my sister asked, "Who are you? I don't know what is going on with you or what you need to do, but you need to get yourself together and talk to God!" She said it in such a way that it took me back to the seventeen-year-old girl who didn't have a clue. I was thirty, at this point, and I felt as helpless as I did as a teenager.

This is the point that I realized that I had deeper issues that I had to uproot before things got too deep. In the midst of all this craziness between Kevin and I, I was able to hide our fighting from my dad. I was so scared to tell him what was going on for multiple reasons, but mainly because I was so embarrassed. I did not want anyone, not even my dad, to know that I was this broken little girl who didn't know how to build healthy relationships. So my sisters gave me an ultimatum to tell my dad about the ordeal with Kevin or they would. I never told him, but he knew. When we talked, he wasn't angry or upset. He was concerned. Not so much because this happened and I allowed it, but because I felt like I couldn't talk to him about it. During that conversation, it hit me. This was the broken piece of me that had never healed. I thought I was so over the issues I had with my father growing up. Perhaps I buried my "father issues" so deep that I didn't realize they were the root of it all.

In the Beginning

My dad and mom met each other in 1979, and a year later, they married in a beautiful African ceremony in Washington, D.C. My mom was petite in size standing at about 5'4 and around 120 pounds. She had a small afro and caramel brown skin. She was the only child to my grandparents Palmer and Lucy and was very spoiled. My grandmother Lucy was a robust woman around 5'8 in stature and 220 pounds. She wore large glasses, brown well-pressed curls, and brown skin. She was an orphan at the age of eight and was primarily raised by her paternal grandmother until she died and was shipped off to live with her aunt. My grandmother was like my best friend growing up. I was her youngest granddaughter, her special present who arrived for her sixtieth birthday. Having a birthday one day before hers gave us this inseparable bond. My grandma

The Material Girl

Lucy understood my wit and candidness, and she never told me to "be quiet" when I said things outlandish yet real. She allowed me to have a voice that should never have been suppressed or withheld from the world. I believe that she gave me this freedom because I was a lot like her. We told things as they were, even if we were undiplomatic and unapologetic.

We shared a commonality: the need for the truth. Since it seemed like everybody else was smoke and mirrors and hid behind the realities of life, we felt the need to bring light to the truth. I can remember my grandmother telling me about my mother and father's wedding. One day, she, my sister, and I were going through some portraits of my parents' wedding. I guess I was around fifteen or so, and we stumbled across a picture of my mother hunched over and my grandmother whispering in her ear. My sister and I were curious, "What were you saying to mom?" One of us asked. She twisted her head to look at the photo and gave us a blank stare as if she was about to break it down to us. She said, "That she can come home WHENEVER she wanted!" We all burst into laughter because we all knew how that story ended! Not long after having me, my mother did in fact return home to my grandparents' home where she started to build her life up after leaving my dad.

The story behind my parents' breakup is equivocal and unsettling, because neither one of their stories line up. They also never took the time to talk to my sister and I about our family structure growing up. It was as if they didn't realize how their actions directly affected our understanding of life. As I've grown older, I have been able to comfortably share my feelings with my parents as to how their decisions, whether selfish or selfless, affected my outlook on life. Parents often fail to warn us about how their bad decisions can affect us. I believe this is partially because they are embarrassed and have to deal with the consequences themselves. I find it disheartening that many parents do not believe that they owe their children an explanation about their decisions. Overtime, I grew to hate my father because I did not see him often, and the only memories that permeated in my mind were when he came to punish me. I remember more of the bad times with him than the good. I am not suggesting that my father wasn't there for me and he wasn't a good father. However, his absence hardened my heart and I grew to feel neglected.

Although he doesn't agree with me, I believe my mom was a single mother. We would see my dad over the weekends, but I spent the majority of my childhood with my mom. She was the parent who took me to Girl Scout meetings and dance practices. She was the backstage parent and the one who helped other kids when we went camping. She and my maternal grandparents are who made memories with my sister and I. It's sad, but I can remember my fifth birthday party, but I can't remember my father being there, however I'm sure he was. Turning five was a big deal so I begged my mom to throw me a birthday party. My birthday is on December 2nd and so close to the holidays, so it was not always fun. The financial burden that came with Christmas coupled with me always wanting a party, because I was such a socialite, created added pressure for my mom. Nonetheless, she made it happen. I remember getting my hair pressed out and curled. I wore a pretty black and pink dress with a pearl necklace and pearl earrings. My god father lived in a complex that had a clubhouse so my mom asked him to rent out the facility for me. I had a DJ, birthday decorations, and plenty of guests. I can recall dancing the day away. With every visitor that arrived, I would make a big deal, give them a hug, thank them for coming, and force them to come and dance with me. My mom always mentions how everyone gleamed about how much of a good host I was at such a young ag. Making all my guests feel important and special was important to me. That day went by so fast.

The Material Girl

The only memory that I have of my dad is him showing up late, as usual, making a big deal about it being his "baby girl's" birthday and being the loudest one signing happy birthday. I don't remember if he stayed the whole time, helped my mom clean up, or even contributed to the festivities. At that point, I think I had become accustom to him being in and out, and so I never held on to the desire of wanting him there.

For some reason, I have blocked him out. With so much tension, you can probably imagine that by the time I became an unruly teenager, the relationship between my father and I didn't exist. It's not like he didn't try. However, it was too late. When I was much younger, I needed him in a different way than my siblings. Since he wasn't there, I built up a defense mechanism. It was as if for every dance recital he missed—and believe me, there were plenty—and every awards assembly when he had to work, I built up a higher wall. Even for the milestones that my father actually attended, he is only a faint memory.

My relationship with him had major effects on me. I considered my natural father so irrelevant to my life that it caused me to feel the same way about my Heavenly Father. The first male relationship that I had wasn't healthy. I tried to convince myself that I didn't need him when I really did. I made his opinion insignificant and the role he played in my life—void. Although he is partly at fault, I determined his significance in my life, and by the age of thirteen, the anger-hurt-resentment had caused me to no longer care whether or not I had a father. Thinking about this now hurts my heart because I so love and adore my dad. Even though we still have our challenges, I believe we have a respect for each other that has grown over time. The breakdown of our relationship was a pinnacle in how I interacted with men. At sixteen and seventeen, I had no model for how a man should treat me. One thing I was sure of, however, was that no man would be allowed to cheat on me like my father had done. Nor would I tolerate someone who did not provide. Unbeknownst to me, my father continued to help my mom financially, but all I saw was a once married woman, now single and making it happen on her own. No matter how dysfunctional our family structure, I can admit that my parents and extended mothers never exposed us children to any friction that may have existed. My mom and dad always got along and they are still like best friends to this day. (This gets weird sometimes, but it's my family.) In fact, my entire family, including my step brothers get together on a consistent basis to celebrate the holidays and each other's milestones.

Reflection: Killing the Weeds

It was tough growing up without my father in the household, but things happen. I always wish I could have been that daddy's girl, clinging on to him for dear life every time he left the house or waiting for him at the door when he arrived home from work. But that's not my story. I had two parents who made some good and some not so good decisions that affected not only themselves, but their families. I wasn't dealt the worst hand; I just didn't live in the house with a picket fence, but who really does? I learned quickly how everything that looks good isn't always good. Even though I wanted my dad there more growing up, I was well provided for and loved by both parents. Even more so, I had lots of family that cared for me, loved me, and helped nurture me. After I got out of that daunting relationship and realized how many issues I still had with men, I sought help. I realized that I no longer could mask the pain of that young girl and went to a therapist. I had that hard conversation with my dad about how I felt when I was younger and how I felt now (when we spoke) about our relationship. I didn't know how to be loved by a man or how to receive love from a man because I had closed myself off to the man who had birthed me. I had become so ice cold towards him to protect myself, so that I didn't feel like a helpless little girl who didn't feel loved by her father.

I had cut myself off, from not only being hurt, but from being loved. The reason why I kept encountering these horrific relationships was because I became accustomed to pain, maybe I was even drawn to it. Now knowing this issue, what was I to do to rectify the situation? To this day, I still struggle with letting my father in. Even writing this book has made me reexamine our relationship to figure out how we fix it. I am still guarded towards my father, and I truly don't always allow him to show me affection, and most of the times, it feels weird and unnatural. It was even tough to share that I am writing this book with him. I tell my mom practically everything, but with my dad, I always feel like he is going to judge me or tell me I'm wrong or can't do it. I am fighting with a person who has all along been in my corner. In my mind, he has always been the tyrant that I would always prove wrong. However, the conversations about my book have brought us closer and given me a lot of insight into what things we still need to work on to build our relationship. Even though at times he doesn't realize it, I really want to have a strong relationship with him, and after our most recent conversation, I have made a decision to work on breaking down the barriers between us.

The revelation of my deep rooted "daddy issues" was a blessing. Instead of consistently falling in a downward spiral, I sought mental and spiritual help. I didn't wallow in the pain. I sought after a solution to eradicate the problem. I had to kill the weeds that were trying to grow in the beautiful garden God had created. To do this, I had to first acknowledge the weeds that existed within my life. I am okay with speaking about them and finding a way to address them every day.

What You Wear Can't Conceal Who You Are

You have already created a pull list as well as the actions that you want to incorporate in your life to get rid of those unhealthy habits. Now it's time to address those weeds. What is the root cause of the lying or cheating? Why do you feel the need to always be the center of attention? Do some digging and writing, reflections are only beneficial to those who are honest with themselves. If you are truly interested in killing the weeds you have to go to places that you may have buried. It may not come to you right away, but write about the experiences you've had with the lying and cheating. Look back at your upbringing and find that one common denominator. Sometimes you need to seek outside help like I did. Depression can be crippling to the mind and your body. Don't be too prideful to seek the proper help because this one "thing" could be keeping you from propelling in to the good life God has laid up for you.

The Material Girl

The Weeds

Chapter 7
My Family Tree

My family tree is quite different than the average family, to say the least. I have such a blended family that I get confused at times about how many siblings I have. I view my father as a ladies' man, but he is also compassionate, caring, and intellectually sound. These attributes played a major part in the decisions he made and the family he has today. However, his upbringing wasn't quite traditional, and after hearing him break down his story, it's quite unnerving if you ask me. My father was born the only child to a sergeant in the army from Louisiana (Robert) and a wealthy southern girl (Mae) from Tennessee.

Now it's a little fussy as to how his parents met, especially since they had totally different upbringings. However, it is clear that my dad nor his father were always treated fairly. My great grandmother Beth was "mean," as my father recalls. She wanted nothing to do with my dad—her grandchild, because of my granddad (his father).

My grandad was brown skin like a walnut. He was considered "lower class." My grandmother was fair-skinned with golden brown finely curled hair. She was from an extremely wealthy fam-

The Material Girl

ily. My father believes his grandmother (my paternal grandmother's mom) disliked him because of his skin complexion. During those times, Jim Crow laws were so heavily enforced and the fear of how my grandmother may be treated because of my grandfather's complexion, could have been one of her fears. My father doesn't really know why there was animosity between his dad and maternal grandmother and never had the opportunity to find out. During those times, the color of your skin and race mattered. Although slavery had been abolished, America was still recouping from the Civil War, and there was still a misconception that "white was right." Many black people even thought this way. My great grandmother was a product of her times and may have had good reasons for her concerns; or perhaps, other factors provoked her dislike for my grandfather that my father may not have known. Either way, it created an uncomfortable situation for my father growing up.

However, as my father described my great grandmother it makes it hard for me to understand her position on race. She herself was a black woman with long silky hair and brown Mohican skin. I imagine that either her daddy or granddaddy was a white slave master, since back in the days, that wasn't uncommon. My father explains that she was a black and Native American woman, who married a white man, my great grandfather Edward. My father doesn't seem to remember much about Edward, but I am aware that he passed himself off as mulatto. We have searched through our family tree to try to uncover all that we could about my dad's grandparents' relationship, however papers were lost and it seems my great grandfather's identity was hidden due to the laws against interracial marriages. However, we learned that my great grandfather had a twin, who eventually started a taxi company, which during those times, were the horses and buggies. I don't know what my great grandfather was like, but I can only imagine a husky white guy, who stood tall and handsome with brown hair and light eyes,

What You Wear Can't Conceal Who You Are

full of life and a deep love for a woman for whom he'd risk his own life. I only say this because any man willing to take the abuse and scrutiny that black people endured at that time to marry and raise children with a black woman had to be one who loved hard and who would make any sacrifice to be with the woman he loved.

Since my great grandfather was born with Kennedy as his last name, there has even been speculations that my great grandfather was a distant cousin to the late President John F. Kennedy. I'm not sure how true that is, but I find my family tree interesting. My dad is a talker and a storyteller of sorts, so he'd always share interesting stories about my ancestry. I don't think he intentionally lied about incidents that had transpired, but I do believe he masked many parts of his past that shaped his worldview. With a newfound understanding of how my dad's younger years must have been, I've developed a deep empathy towards my father. In the words of the great *Mother to Son* poem by Langston Hughes, "Life for [him] ain't been no crystal stair"— not even a mere reflection of it. I do not recall my dad mentioning anything about my grandfather Robert's family, but I get the sense that his family hated my grandmother just as much as her family hated him.

A not-so-bright side of my father's past that I've uncovered is the tumultuous household in which he was raised. It was full of fights, arguments, violence, and a lack of care for him at times. My father has such a good heart and a love for people, but what he always lacked, in my opinion, was compassion. I think his foundation for fatherhood was grounded in keeping his children away from an atmosphere of violence and feelings of unsafety. However, although he kept us from violence—he built an environment of insecurity for his family, a world that consisted of one too many woman and several children fighting for his attention. See my dad left his parents' house at the early age of sixteen, not because he wanted to, but because his mother's ongoing battle with bipolar disorder mixed with his father's rage had become unbearable. He was raised in the Catholic church. His mom was a teacher, and I truly enjoyed being around her when I was a youngster. Although this was the complete opposite of what my dad experienced, my grandmother never raised a hand or even her voice at me when I was growing up.

    I share these stories because it is important for us to understand our family histories and where we come from in order to understand ourselves. See life doesn't really just happen. People breathe life into others and live life day-to-day not thinking of how it may affect their children's children. When I finally processed the accounts of my father's upbringing and compared his childhood to my own, I received deep revelations.

    During this time, life had no merit to me. I felt that life wasn't a privilege; it was a disservice. Why was I chosen to live in a day when things mattered more than people and people build relationships based on what they can get? Not to mention, I reasoned that I was in a family that just seemed to be a mess. My daddy was not faithful to my mom; I had multiple siblings by women other than my mom; I had to constantly adjust to the different rules in the different households. I struggled to be noticed in the midst of a crowd of what seemed like a million people, and above all else, I felt like I had to fight for my parents' attention and affection. I mean was this how life was supposed to be? My life had been in the hands of my gatekeepers, my parents, but they had not made the best decisions for their own lives. Unfortunately, their decisions ended up affecting my life in a way they probably didn't understand. This is my perception and only my side of the story, of course. When speaking to my mom and dad they remember things quite differently. They say I was always defiant and rambunctious growing up. I hated hearing the word "no," and despite my inexperience, I fought them on everything.

What You Wear Can't Conceal Who You Are

Now I won't blame anybody for my decisions and life choices, however, too often parents do things around their children assuming their behaviors will not have an effect. The environment in which I was being raised and the assumptions I formed based on my experiences made life seem difficult to handle. I had trusted and believed that my atmosphere was a clear depiction of my future life. I did not like what was in front of me, therefore, I made a decision at a young age that I would do things my way. This attitude probably stemmed from my stubborn and strong-willed personality. Part of me thinks that I also became that way after feeling alone, let down, hurt, abandoned, and unworthy. I decided that I would do things my way since everyone else was doing things their way and didn't care how I felt. So why not do the same? As long as it made me happy, and I wasn't in any real danger, I lived life on my terms. If there was a soundtrack to my life at the time, it would've definitely been "My Prerogative" by Bobby Brown.

"Everybody's talkin all this stuff about me
Why don't they just let me live (Tell me why)
I don't need permission
Make my own decisions (Oh!)
That's my prerogative
It's my prerogative
(It's my prerogative)"
"It's the way that I wanna live (It's my prerogative)
I can do just what I feel (It's my prerogative)
No one can tell me what to do (It's my prerogative)".

Growing up, this song played over and over in my head. It was my posture and my position in life, "just let me live" and do what I want to do. How often do we think that we can just go around living life as we see fit? We think, *so what, I'm not grown, it's my life and I should be able to have complete say in what I can and cannot do.* Like most teenagers, I thought that I should've been in control of my bed time, my actions, my selection of friends, if and when I went to school, and so forth. This thinking doesn't stop as teenagers either. All of us have this sense of entitlement after we are born that suggests, "I was created a free spirit, so let me go and be free." We want to be free from rules, free from burdens and free from responsibility. Ha! Sounds so good, but in reality it's not real. Life is a blessing that not everybody gets to enjoy for long. God has birthed each of us with a purpose. It is our duty to live out our days in complete holiness and look to Him for guidance. We are a spirit, we have a soul, and we live in a body. When we allow our bodies to control our souls (mind, will, and emotions), we suffocate our spirits and kill the original intent God had for us. Before we are formed in our mothers' wombs, God makes it clear that He has already set up shop for us. We have a house to live in (our bodies), a good paying job (our purpose), a friend we can always count on in our times of need (Holy Spirit), and food to eat (the word of God, AKA the bible). The necessities of life have been preordained, and we don't even notice it. However, one of the most crucial parts of all these things working together are "choices," or what I call the BIG "C." A choice is the one thing that God gives us freely, and this free will, or choice, to decide our own actions will ultimately determine our destinies.

Not knowing then what I know now, I decided that since everyone else was making decisions that were beneficial for them, yet affecting me, I too would do the same thing, as long as I was happy in that moment. I didn't care about the long-term effect of my choices beyond my own happiness. That mindset was a slippery slope, and I consistently slid time and time again.

Growing up, life wasn't ideal, but it wasn't all that bad either. I wasn't molested or raped as a child. I was not badly abused, although my father was on the border line of child abuse with some of his beatings. I was never homeless, and I was not without love. I was merely a young (rebellious) girl born into an abnormal family situation, which seemed dysfunctional.

A natural parent can sculpt a child's image of her Heavenly Father without either party knowing it. There came a point in my life when I had to let my father know how I felt, and as hard of a conversation that it was, it birthed and inner peace within me to build a better relationship with him based on love. Again, my father was not completely absent, but he was emotionally absent and often working or caring to other matters, some of which improved our family's lives. Once I confronted my father about my true feelings, we had an opportunity to rebuild a healthier, loving relationship that I needed. Although it is still a work in progress, things are gradually getting better. I am not as defensive as I used to be. I am opening up and sharing things about myself with him, and I am learning more and more about him as time passes.

I am a firm believer that children will do what they see versus what they are told. This is why it's important that parents live lives they wouldn't mind seeing their kids live. It's also important NOT to live a lie. Kids see right through disingenuous adults. They are processing more than their parents think. When my friends or family curse at or around their kids, I always tell them not to be surprised when the children start cursing back. Too often, adults forget how impressionable and cognitive children are in their infancy. I recently read that studies have shown that a "healthy baby will emerge from the womb with 100 billion neurons, nearly twice as many neurons as adults, in a brain that's half the size. This massive number of neurons is necessary for the tremendous amount of learning a baby has to do in its first year of life. While brain volume will double by the age of three, not all of those neurons will stick

The Material Girl

around; synaptic pruning takes place as a baby ages, in which the brain gets rid of weaker synaptic connections in favor of stronger ones." (Source: http://mentalfloss.com/article/70105/10-amazing-facts-about-infant-brain)

The mind of an infant is powerful. When adults fail to realize it, their own actions and the child's environment, shape the brain to have predetermined values about life. Although as a child, my parents instilled very good principles and morals when it came to family, religion, love, compassion, giving, independence, education, discipline, health, and spirituality, I learned nothing about relationships, sex, monogamy, and finances. These have always been my struggle areas, and I realized it was because I was never taught to value them or their importance to life. I may have gotten grilled about not understanding the value of a dollar, but when you get anything you ask for, how can you truly understand? My family attempted to provide guidance in these areas, but by that time, I had already formed my own perceptions simply by observing their actions.

As an adult now, I can no longer blame my parents for my actions and decisions. I grow in these areas by understanding why the deficits exist and working hard to fix them. Change does not just happen overnight. Life is about progression, constantly acknowledging where things went wrong and consistently trying to fix them. It doesn't help when you consistently loop back and make the same dumb decisions. As my pastor likes to say, "You can't do the same things and expect different results!" You have to do something different to get something different and I believe looking over your past history will help you deal with some deeper issues that may haunt you, but also help you move on.

What You Wear Can't Conceal Who You Are

Reflection: My past isn't my future, but it explains A LOT!

I shared my family's past to present a contrast between history and inheritance. The bible talks about the "generational curse." This is unknown repetitive behavior that transcends through time. It's like DNA. You can't see it, but you know it exists. We innately inherit the character flaws and strengths of our ancestors. I found this journey through my past therapeutic. It helped me to see not only what I was doing wrong, but why I was doing it wrong. I didn't know a lot of the information about my dad and my mom's past growing up, and I learned some of it as a result of discussing this book with them. Nonetheless, it was so apparent how important the past is and its relevance to the future. This chapter was one of the hardest to write. I have revealed some of the deepest parts of my insecurities. In exposing myself, I am able to find joy in knowing that I have enough insight to now change my future.

Now it's time for you to go through your family tree. Talk to your parents and family to find out more about your lineage. Where do you come from? Although you have a heavenly father, you also have an earthly father and as much as you don't want to admit it, your earthly father plays a big part in how you maneuver through life. Your issue may not be your dad, but it may have been bouncing from foster home to foster home, never really even having a family or knowing where you are from. Even if you never uncover that information, find peace in knowing that you know your roots and you work every day to kill the weeds. Reflect on what you discover while exploring your family tree.

Reflection: Family Tree................

Chapter 8
Friends or No Friends

February 9, 2012 was a normal day at work, or so I thought. I was in my sixth year of teaching business education in a high school and was also a first year graduate student. Around 12 p.m., midway through my class, I received a phone call from my friend Kelz who never calls me during the day. I just felt the need to answer, because I was curious as to why she was calling at this time. I'll never forget the next few minutes of that day.

I said, "Hey Kelz what's up?" she paused as if she knew I had no idea of what was going on that day in my friend's life.

"Uh hey! You heard about Torre?"

"No why, what happened?" as the concern in my voice elevated.

"Have you talked to Ree today?"

"No, what's going on with Torrean is everything okay?" As soon as the question left my mouth, I was overcome with a feeling of worry.

"Kiana told Mark she was in an accident!"

"Is she okay?"

"I don't know! It was a bad accident! Call Ree!"

The Material Girl

I quickly hung up the phone and stepped outside of my class. I was uncertain what was going on and fear seeped through my entire body. I had no idea what to think. Although all these things happened within seconds of each other, I can remember how I felt in every moment.

Ring... Ring... "Hello!"

"Ree what's going on? Kelz told me Torrean was in an accident. Please just tell me she is okay! REE...," I said as tears started to roll down my cheek, because I knew by the sound of her voice that she wasn't okay.

A pause of silence came over the phone as I held my breath hoping that the words that would come from the other end of the phone would be, "She's fine!"

But there was nothing, not one sound... just air and emptiness...

Then, I heard her cry and I can remember screaming to her, "REE JUST TELL ME SHE IS OKAY PLEASE, JUST SAY SHE'S HERE!"

The next words sent pain through my entire body... "SHE'S GONE!"

My outburst after that was uncontrollable and unclear... I ran from my classroom into the business office trying to find comfort and answers to an insurmountable amount of questions that ran through my head. The scream and gut-wrenching cry after that was something I will never forget. It felt like a part of me no longer existed. The days after that were hard, but also enlightening. I surrounded myself with a bunch of some of our mutual friends and her loved ones. Everyone said nothing but positive things about Torrean and spoke about the impact she had on their lives. I had no clue how it felt to lose a close friend at such a young age. I knew she had a lot to offer the world, yet she would never get an opportunity. I can remember being upset with God. The accident was not her fault and was the result of someone else not paying attention. So how was it that this vivacious young girl with a big heart could be taken from the world before reaching her full potential? And why wasn't I given the chance to get our friendship back on track?

My feelings at that time are such a hard thing to explain because Torrean and I had not been as close as we were in previous years. The last year and a half, we had a distance between us because of some of our life choices. We had just recently been in communication, and a month earlier we had set up a time to hangout for Martin Luther King Jr. Day, but neither one of us followed up. While grieving, I constantly beat myself up, because our last interaction was a text telling her we have to reschedule our date.

Although we weren't together every week like in times past, I missed her. I missed her consistent presence in my life and the endless sleepovers and home beauty shop sessions we use to have. We weren't on bad terms or mad at each other, our friendship just went in different directions because of the relationship she was in the previous year. I wasn't mad at her for being with this guy. I was disappointed in the decision she made, because she deserved so much more. I felt like this guy took my friend away and took a piece of her dignity as well. The main reason for the distance was because I told her how I felt about their relationship and the decision they made to live with each other prior to being married. I was lucky to have spoken with her about this and hashed out the situation prior to her death. We both apologized to the other for our individual roles in the diminishment of the friendship.

I was a little resentful towards her because she was my crutch when I became saved and began learning God's way of living holy. She was the only person who I saw as cute and fly, but who also lived a life of standards and morals beyond what her mother and father taught her. She reverenced God like no one I knew at the time we met as eighteen-year-old college freshmen. I not only looked up to her for guidance, but I really needed her for support. She was not like the typical church people that stuck their noses in the air when someone did something wrong. Torre could give her friends the gut-wrenching truth and then invite us out to the mall for lunch. Her spirit was so pleasant and loving, but her truth was spiritual. She could also hold a secret that not even God could get out of her.

As time moved on, things changed and by the time we were twenty-eight-years old our relationship changed. I'm not sure if over time she grew tired of living righteously, but it was like our roles had reversed. She wasn't perfect, but she lived her life with such high standards that everyone around her—both young and old— had to respect it. She herself even explained to me the turmoil she went through in the relationship that broke us apart and told me she really needed to come back to church and redirect her life.

Despite her choices, she was still an honorable friend. One of the last times that we hung out, I mentioned wanting to go to the club with her, and she said told me "no," because I didn't need to expose myself to that atmosphere. As usual, I complied and told her she was right. I still couldn't understand how she was once in my shoes and had become comfortable in these settings. I always wonder if I should have prayed more or reached out more to get her back into the word like she would always do for me. Don't get me wrong, she always loved having a good time and enjoying life, but some things were different about her, and I didn't know how to be the friend to help her as she had done for me.

I told her that I didn't like her choices, but my concern only created distance between us. When you tell your friends what you think about their decisions, no matter how much you love them, and even if your intent is pure, it may cause friction. When this hap-

What You Wear Can't Conceal Who You Are

pens, I always think about the biblical principle: light cannot live with darkness, and those who make negative or bad choices will no longer want to hang out with someone who doesn't condone those decisions. Most often people cannot handle their friends being honest. In reality, people want honesty as long as they're comfortable, others are cheering them on, or participating in the same types of activities. Oftentimes, friendships dissipate when two people choose different directions, and longtime friendships sink when one person changes, elevates, or tries to mature and live for God. I don't think this happens on purpose. I think it's like a subconscious thing that people do to avoid feeling less than or inadequate. This is not to say a person is bad, because he or she made bad decisions. It's human nature to feel uncomfortable doing wrong when someone calls us out about living right. They may question the friendship or reject the challenge to "level up." I've learned that discomfort is essential to our daily lives. If we're not uncomfortable, that means we're not growing, being stretched, and being pushed into our full potential. Anything that grows goes through a period of discomfort. Growth requires a stretching and all of us need to surround ourselves with people that are going to give us that feeling of discomfort. It's dangerous to hang around people who allow us to settle in our current states, because life is not just about being steady, it is also about progression and growth. Every day of life should be a learning lesson. We should grow each day, so it's important to be surrounded by people who are going to consistently push us to new levels. My pastor will always tell the congregation, "If you show me your friends, I can predict your future." When I first became saved, I prioritized this principle in prayer, because I knew that I wasn't surrounded by people who wanted to live life like I did.

The Material Girl

How things were

Prior to my friendship with Torre, everyone around me was materialistic. They all looked like me, talked like me, and I had no one around who could show me anything different. The late 90's and early 2000's started an era of social acceptance and materialism amongst my group of peers. During this time, social media and the Internet became easier to access and communication via instant messenger or chat rooms began to form what we see today as the social media frenzy. During this time, there was a struggle amongst teenagers to be accepted and appear successful by the things we possessed, although most of us relied heavily on our parents' income and resources. Looking back now, I feel this was utterly stupid because of the mere fact that all of us were living in the same middle-class area with parents who worked to provide for us. No one came from multi-million-dollar families, but rather, in most cases, our parents earned no more than $60,000 a year. Even my mom, who climbed her way up the success latter within her agency, made six figures, yet still struggled to provide for two growing teenagers. The entertainment industry influenced the thinking of my generation.

During the 90's, hip-hop was on the rise, and rappers often made songs about the finer things in life, even if they were just a facade. Two focuses of my generation and the current one are money and sex. Even though I'm not or never was that big into rap, I was still influenced by the culture. From Lil Kim, who flaunted her 'sex-capades' and made them a symbol of female empowerment, as if she (and women like her) were in complete control, to Notorious B.I.G. who rapped about his experiences selling drugs in NYC, it was as if we were all eating from a poisonous tree whose fruit appeared to be ripe and appetizing.

What You Wear Can't Conceal Who You Are

Listening to others

I had no one around who could help redirect my focus from this strong influence. When I dated guys because of the perception that they had money or materialistic things, I did what was expected because everyone around me did the same things. Even now, I have to talk to some of the young ladies in my school about the appearance of money and how dating at their age should never be about selling themselves, because of what a guy may or may not have. I tell them to look at dating for money as a form of prostitution. Some may think my approach is extreme, but I think it's sad that young women are willing to lose their virginity because a boy is able to buy them nice things or take them out to eat. It's a clear case of identity crisis—many females do not understand their value. This will allow a person to be easily persuaded to do things that puts him or her in a bad situation. Nonetheless, I was surrounded by carbon copies—a bunch of people who looked, acted, and sounded like me. I even look around today and see some of the same people that were considered "popular," back then, including former friends who I parted ways with, still trying to keep up appearances while struggling to pay bills, still living with their parents, with no financial plan or savings. These same people are on social media acting as if life is great.

"Friendships" during my teenage years were unstable, unreliable, and unhealthy. We were extremely codependent on each other's acceptance and did things to impress our so-called friends. I always felt like the odd man out when it came to my opinions and the way I perceived life. Often, I would suppress my opinions, depending on who I was listening to and what other people thought. Listening to other's viewpoints on things made me become like them. I was a virgin up until tenth grade, and I was fine with that. However, the over sexualized media and the conversations around me about what sex was like and that girls had to have sex to keep guys, convinced me to act on those influences. I couldn't gather my own position because my ear was so focused on what other people were saying. Listening to others was a big issue for me. The girl who I really was constantly fought against the woman I was becoming.

I didn't look inward for answers or even pick up a book to find out the truth on the topics we discussed. The only information I gathered came from my group of friends. I have experienced a lot of friendships that have stirred me in different directions, however I didn't really understand the importance of friendships until I was saved.

Finding my voice

By the time I was in the circle with "the popular kids," I started to find my own voice. I started to appreciate my aggressive, yet high saditty attitude, which made me feel superior to others. I realized that going against the grain wasn't that bad after all, especially because I could manipulate people easily. I always liked to be in charge and lead others, but as I grew older, it became a battle of the teens, and whoever had the most minions won. Often, I lost this battle, because I wasn't the nicest person and I had a smart, not-to-mention, hostile mouth. Instead of leading by example and building character, I succumbed to the "it" factor. I tried to be "it" so badly that I ultimately became a carbon copy of everyone else.

When I started to notice that people were admiring me (after I started dressing a certain way and changed my attitude) I became an arrogant chick. It turned a lot of people off. Instead of being a caring person who welcomed other people, my demeanor was like 'who are you?" I had created a persona of the girl who had it all together. It made me feel like no matter what anyone said, I had the

What You Wear Can't Conceal Who You Are

upper hand. Why? I don't know. To this day, I think it had a lot to do with me trying to sell a position.

By the end of my tenth grade year, I had changed, and my outlook on friendships were different. This shift occurred after an unexpected breakdown in multiple friendships. God has a crazy way of allowing things to break you down so that He is there to restore what was lost or not there to begin with. The best part of this story is the ending and my present day relationships with some of the same people. I have stayed so focused on staying on my path of righteousness that the relationships that were at one point in shambles are healthy and fruitful now. This didn't happen overnight of course. It was a process. I prayed for my friends when I didn't want to. I stood on my faith in areas that helped to positively influence them. I had hard conversations about issues within the friendships, and I walked away when the friendships weren't fruitful (whether because of me or the other person).

Above all, I remained consistent. As a matter of fact, two of my friends in particular kept asking me about what I was going to say about them in my book, because they didn't want to have to sue me for defamation LOL, (which was a joke, and a good one at that). See they have been with me throughout this journey and have witnessed most, if not all, of the accounts in this book. Although they have been a part of some of my downfalls, they too have been around for many of my defining moments in life and helped me through tough times by reminding me of who I am. They weren't super saved and spiritual, but they held me accountable to the person I had openly vowed that I wanted to become. The truth is that every relationship comes with growing pains and difficult moments, but the best relationships withstand the tests of time and eventually blossom. So I'll say to these friends, "Thanks for the journey, the good, the bad, and the ugly." Even the rough spots created special moments. The process isn't the reward; it's the promise that keeps our faith. I learned that from my pastor.

When going through a situation, things can seem daunting and frustrating. However, looking at the reward or promise attached to the process makes it easier to endure. For instance, people go to college every day. Higher education comes with many challenges, from financial to the academic. Despite it all, people pay money because they know if they stay on the right path and finish, they can expect a degree, which could help open doors for them in the future. This promise is enough to uphold them through the process.

True Friendship God's Way

It's important to understand the foundational principles of a relationship. Having a relationship with God has helped me to have discernment when entering or removing myself from different friendships. God places people in your life that serve a purpose, however, sometimes these people can be seasonal. Having clarity and (most importantly) peace within these relationships are crucial to your growth and maturity. So to say I had no clue how to discern relationships when I was younger is an understatement. I *was* who I hung around!

You may have a really good friend who is a little wild and very promiscuous. I can almost guarantee you that even if you don't start out that way, you will either be labeled like her because you are around her and accept her behavior, or you will start acting like her. This principle is very important to understanding life; it doesn't just apply to friendships. It is a Godly principle that will help direct you. What you lend your ears and eyes to become your habits. **Mark 4:24** says, "Take heed what you hear. With the same measure you use, it will be measured to you; and to you who hear, more will be given."

In addition, **Psalm 101:3** says, "I will set nothing wicked before my eyes; I hate the work of those who fall away; It shall not cling to me." Whatever you tolerate, through your ears or your actual presence will become true in your life as well. It's important to realize the influence that friends have on your life and your future and to guard what comes into your eyes and ears.

Reflection: You are who you hang around

Through the good and bad friendships, I learned a lot about myself. I found out that I would rather lead than follow, that building good friendships are hard work, some friendships are seasonal, your friends can build you up or break you down, and friendship should grow with you in life.

In the midst of me examining my friendships, I also found that I wasn't as good of a friend as I thought I was. As a matter of fact, I was altogether bad at relationships. I always wanted to be right, or I felt like my opinions matter most. At times, I voiced my opinions when they weren't desired or received well at all. This created turmoil in my friendships that neither benefitted me or my friends. Since I desired and cried out to God for healthy friendships, He made me first examine the type of friend I was to other people. He was perfecting the things in me with every turn down my path. Like with every other thing in life, I did what I wanted versus what was beneficial to all parties involved. My friendships became about me instead of "us". While God was working on me, I had to focus on me versus talking about them. If I could be a better friend than I have the right to expect a good friend.

This revelation became the foundational principle I still stand on today in regards to relationships. I can only expect to receive what I am capable of supplying. With acknowledging my flaws in this area, I was able to attract healthier relationships overtime and even rebuild old ones. Friendships are important to life and if they are nurtured can be a blessing. In order for you to build healthy friendships you must first be the friend you want in your life, you must seek out people who think like you (not act like you), be willing to work through disagreements, and value your differences. I have so many valuable friendships in my life today. I don't talk to my friends every day, but I pray for all of them daily. I don't just pray when things are going wrong, but I pray that they can have the life God set before them. I hold them accountable, but I've learned tact when approaching them. If you do not have these types of friendships, you should probably look in the mirror first before looking at other people, because every improvement in your life must start with you.

    Start by journaling your ideal friendship the same way you would journal your ideal relationship with the opposite sex. Describe what type of friendship you want and compare it to the friendships you have. If things don't match up, you have work to do. Now don't go to your friends talking about, "I have to cut you off because you are not lining up to my friendship goals!" Just take notes of the unhealthy things that exist in your friendships. Overtime, talk to them about the things you want to change and if they aren't receptive to these issues, walk away. I have literally told some of my friends that I felt as though our friendships weren't fruitful. Some stuck around and some faded away. As a matter of fact, the same friends that I mentioned to you earlier in the chapter said that they would sue me if I talked bad about them in the book. One friend that I had that conversation with is still here today and our friendship is better than it has ever been. Although we have known each other since middle school, we had grown to be very different people. We never talked about the changes, we just acted as if every thing was okay. However, it wasn't. We had changed, but our friendship hadn't. Even though I didn't have the best approach in telling her, because she found out from another mutual friend, she was receptive and even apologized for how I may have felt. I too had to apologize for not coming to her sooner. It didn't change our friendship overnight, but because we valued each other, we worked on it. I worked on understanding her more and she did the same. Now we have a really strong friendship, where we help and hold each other accountable. She won't let me date any guy because she knows I'm waiting until marriage, and I hold her accountable to her career goals. Friends are important to success. So never stop building friendships and allowing them to evolve. Always remember that you are who you hang around, so hang around those who have your answers and get away from those who have your problem.

The Material Girl

Friends No Friends
(Journal what Your Ideal Friendship Would Look Like)

Chapter 9
Power

Here I am lined up, dressed in my black gown, purple stole, and black hat, tassel pulled to the side, standing tall and waiting for the music to start. The music is cued and the pomp and circumstance begins. All twenty plus graduates are excited and ready to begin our graduation, which some did not make it to see. This is not the typical graduation day from a college or university; it is the end of my journey at the Spirit of Faith Bible Institute. After three long years, today, June 12, 2011, I am graduating with a diploma in ministerial studies. This day means so much to me for a multitude of reasons. I have worked so hard to get here, but the past that I left behind doesn't seem that far away.

~

As I prepared myself to get ready for graduation, I wanted to make sure my hair and makeup were done, and every stitch was in its rightful place. So before walking out the door, I stopped and looked in the mirror and smiled, showing all thirty-two teeth, I exhaled and told myself, "You did it!" My mind instantly traveled back to that day of March in 2001 when I didn't know my identity.

The Material Girl

Now, there I was ready to graduate from a Bible institute after I'd already graduated from college and began working in a career that I loved (and I had excelled in that career, might I add). The girl I saw that day was totally different than the girl I was ten years prior who was afraid, ashamed, and didn't know herself. She was caught-up in the bags, the clothes, and material things. But on this day, my graduation day, the reflection in the mirror was a woman, clothed in His righteousness, covered by His love, and walking in her purpose. My life had changed from the material girl to the Woman with the Material. Packing wisdom, knowledge, and Holy Spirit, I knew I was a woman who had the favor of God upon my life and I had taken the time to find out who I am in Him. This day I stood strong and proud of my accomplishments. The fact that I endured, but persevered, through times of struggle was an accomplishment, and I made sacrifices to get to the day when I could say I not only graduated from college, but earned a diploma in ministerial studies. Moreover, I knew who I was and was okay with it. I had learned to take on the challenges in the world one day at a time, with my Bible and notebook in tow. I learned to record the journey ahead and was willing to read for insight and wisdom, and I understood that I was (am) nothing without Him.

As the program began, words of wisdom and encouragement were spoken into our lives from multiple teachers, ministers, and pastors who had walked with us throughout the journey of school. All of us were smiling ear-to-ear, so proud of what we had overcome. Now this was not my first graduation. I had graduated from high school in 2001 and received my bachelor's degree in marketing in 2005. But this graduation was different; the atmosphere was one that reverenced God's presence and was encouraging to do God's work in the earth. I remember the song the psalmist sung, "I Give Myself Away" by William McDowell. This song was so fitting for this ceremony. Most of the graduates stood with our hands lifted.

What You Wear Can't Conceal Who You Are

Tears began flowing from my eyes—these were not tears of sadness, rather tears of joy, because I had made an oath to serve God in everything I would do, which seemed daunting. My tears told my story; I was an overcomer. I was so happy that despite my bad decisions and awful choices, God still saw it fit to restore me and allow me to serve Him. My life was not perfect by any means, but I had redirected my negative thoughts to a place where I only saw light in the midst of darkness. I was grateful. I was humble, and most of all, I was happy. The same girl who felt so defeated and as if she had the weight of the world on her shoulders years ago, was now a woman of purpose secure in who I had become. That day I was getting ready to embark on a journey that would propel my life to the next level. This day signified more than just a graduation in obtaining a diploma in ministerial studies, but was a day that marked the life of a survivor destined for greatness. Later that evening, after the speakers and singers completed their respective roles, I walked across the stage, shook hands, took pictures, and greeted my loved ones who had come.

The road to get to that point was not that fun. As I think back to my thirteen-year-old self to that very moment, I had been trying to figure out why I was on earth. Now it all made sense; I was born to overcome and to testify. My life was not just about me. It was about the people I would encounter and meet throughout life. It was about the moment I struggled to the moment I persevered so I could look back and grab the next person's hand to bring them along. The power existed in me the entire time; I just didn't know how to use it. Now I was equipped, locked and loaded. Not only was I smart, but I was knowledgeable. I had a clear line of connection with the Creator, and I could go to him and receive all that I needed. I had been taught through this process how to use Holy Spirit as my helper. The last missing ingredient to the puzzle, I so carefully sought out, had been put into its rightful place.

The Material Girl

Now I don't say this to push everyone to attend a bible institute or college. However, this is my truth, my enlightenment, and my puzzle piece. That day in March sparked such a fire in me and lit a desire to find myself and my purpose. Since I was so diligently committed to this, I found answers for my life. What I've learned about God is that He is always there and ready to be used by his creations, but He waits for us to pull the trigger. He has all of the answers to life locked up in a special box created for each individual person but many don't know what's in that box because they never asked. Let's just say that I asked and He answered, time after time after time.

The Road to Get There

The road getting to this solace place wasn't easy and the time since then has not been easy either. Right before I graduated from college, I was so lost. I had made college my identity for four years and when it was time to graduate, I had to find a career to which I could identify. Towards the end of my senior year in college, I remember going to church one Sunday and hearing a lesson about "purpose." I felt like God Himself had come from above and was in the pulpit talking to me because, He knew I was not certain of my purpose. That Monday, as I pulled up to school, thoughts of what I would do in the next few months before graduation were working my brain. What job should I look for? Do I want to just get an MBA? Should I move to an area with more opportunities in business? What am I supposed to do? God help me! It was time to get a job and I was clueless, even more unsure of what I was supposed to do than when I entered college. I was working an internship at a news station that I didn't particularly care for and I thought it was boring. I had a summer job lined up, but after that, I had nothing. I called out that day and asked God, "What is my purpose? What am I supposed to be doing on this earth?" Right after the last word came out of my mouth I heard, "teaching." Now this was weird because it was my first encounter with hearing or knowing the difference between me talking to myself and hearing from the inner being which Christians call "Holy Spirit." This voice was very similar to my own and what everybody calls your "self-conscious." So in response, I burst out into laughter, and said, "Yeah right! They don't make enough money for me, and wait! I just went to school for business. I'm not giving these people no more of my money to get a second degree in teaching." In that moment, I dismissed the very notion of me becoming a teacher and proceeded to the next ideas. However, this moment would come back up again in the near future, as only a reminder that God is who He is today, tomorrow, and for eternity.

Months after that moment, I had graduated, finished working my summer job, went on countless interviews, and was now jobless. This was a hard time for me. I had gone to school for marketing and loved the creative aspect of it, but I hated the sales side. All the entry level positions available to me at that time were in sales. I turned down some jobs, and I bombed various others. Instead of selling myself, I told them the honest truth. I wasn't good at sales and probably wouldn't do my best in bringing in revenue for the company. Well I didn't say things like that, but I said enough for them to count me out for those positions. However, I had enough understanding of the word at that time that I knew I should still have hope. Since my grandmother's health was failing, I would help my mom by taking her to and from dialysis and she would give me a little money to cover some of my expenses. I also would tutor throughout the week to help pay the remainder of my bills. After six months had passed with no job, I began to feel discouraged, so I prayed. During that time, I was talking to my ex-boyfriend Roger's mother. Although he and I hadn't been together for years, we remained friends and I was very close to his family. So his mom

The Material Girl

suggested I fill out an application to substitute at her job. She worked for a school with students with special needs as an aide and they needed people to come in and work from time-to-time. That next week, she was able to get me an interview with her principal. The principal explained the process for working there and instructed me to fill out an application online. Unbeknownst to me, this application was not to just work in that school, but to substitute anywhere in the county. So right after I went through all the training, I was called to substitute for a high school where my little cousins attended. I took the assignment because I felt that I was earning a few dollars for babysitting big kids, and I could also keep an eye on my cousins. The first day was nerve-racking. The teacher posted instructions for the assignment, and I did my best to keep these teenagers occupied. I was only twenty-two and was still a baby myself. I looked even younger than I was at that time and teachers constantly asked me for hall passes when I went into the halls. I was asked to come back again the following week. The second day on the job, I had more confidence than before. Although the first time I had a class of about five to ten kids at a time, this time I had classes of thirty teenagers. I didn't think about it at the time, but God knew exactly what to do to get me to a place so that He could reveal His intended purpose for my life. He knew that if I had over thirty kids in my classroom on the first day, I would have never returned the second time. I had just enough confidence from my first experience to carry through to the next.

    I didn't let the students run over me. I told them they needed to remain in their seats unless they asked to go to the bathroom. I nicely asked them to keep the noise down. Every once in a while, I would walk around, ask if anyone needed help, and I instructed them to lower their voices. I was lucky to have subbed for math classes; I was really good in math and confident in my ability to teach the students. This day wasn't as easy as the previous one. I realized that there was always at least one student in each class who would try to intimidate me or test my patience. However, since I was once their age and fairly hip on the language at the time, I would use the authority I had been given by the administration to threaten them with some type of discipline. They learned quickly that I was down-to-earth but very serious about the job I had been given, and they respected me.

Throughout the day, a fellow teacher, who looked as if she was ready to pop, would waddle her pregnant self across the hall to stop by and check on them. She looked fairly young herself, maybe twenty-five, and Ethiopian, very small in stature and friendly. Every time she stopped by, she would tell me that she was surprised at how obedient and settled the kids had been while I was there. She mentioned to me that I had kept the kids in better condition than their actual teacher. At the end of the day, she came in to tell me how impressed she was with my ability to maintain order and at my young age. She asked me a little about myself and I told her I was a recent graduate, working there while trying to find a job. She asked if I would substitute for her classroom while she was out the next week and I obliged. Shortly after I stood in for her, she reached out to me and asked if I would stay until the end of the year. She would be going on maternity leave until the following school year. I again said yes and started my journey as a teacher.

Her class was more than I had bargained for, with no formal teaching experience, I did what I could to keep them tamed. I used my power over the boys (all the young boys would drool over me) to get them to do what I needed for them to remain focused, and I appealed to the girls' desire to be my friend, since I was young and hip. This class was tough. I had ninth grade students who were all in remedial math because of their behavior or attendance problems or their inability to understand basic algebra. I took this job serious

The Material Girl

and I loved it. I enjoyed teaching so much that I requested a meeting with the principal close to the end of the year to discuss my return. God reminded me that he had already purposed me to teach. Now it was my job to figure out how and where.

Initially I thought I was going to teach math. I spoke to my uncle about it and he being extremely wise said, "Although God called you to be a teacher, He will also give you the desires of your heart, so if you love business, why would he make you teach math? You may be called to teach people in the business world!" That made me think; I remembered taking accounting and a business management class in high school, which is the reason I pursued a degree in that field to begin with. *Why not look for teaching jobs in business*, I thought. A light bulb went off. I started researching, and that summer, while working my summer job, I applied in the Prince George County School System, since I was already substituting there. They told me I needed another business class, so I enrolled in graduate classes at a local college to get those credits during the summer. Once I brought back my transcript, I knew God would open up a door for me to start teaching there, but I was surprised when the lady from human resources instructed me that there were no jobs available in business that upcoming school year. Feeling defeated, I went to my mom and cried telling her all about how I knew God told me to do this, but I felt like the door had closed *after* I finally felt like I knew what I was purposed for. She reminded me that my God father had a friend who worked as a principal in Baltimore County and to give him a call and see what he could do. Little did I know, my mom had it all confused. He worked in an entirely different county in Maryland. However, God knew exactly what He was doing and used my mother as a vessel to get me to where I needed to go. Nonetheless, I went to my summer job office and prayed. "God my tears are not because I don't believe you, but because I'm frustrated and don't know what to do."

What You Wear Can't Conceal Who You Are

"I know what you told me and I have faith that you will make it happen for me, but I'm scared and confused and I need you." I heard Him tell me not to wait to hear back from my God father's friend, but to go on the website and contact the hiring office. It's amazing how when you feel like your back is against the wall you think outside the box. I think these moments build true character and shows you how resourceful you can be in times a doubt. So I wiped my tears, went online, and called the office. I didn't just call Baltimore County's office, but I called all the school systems in a twenty-mile radius. I was not going to let one "no" be the final answer. A "no" today doesn't mean "no" tomorrow. So I searched for my "yes," the only way I knew how, by hustling. "Hi, my name is Mudiwa Johnson, and I am a recent college graduate with a degree in marketing. I have some teaching experience and am interested in a business education job in your county. Do you know who I need to speak with?" The young lady patched me in to the hiring manger's line. He told me to fax my resume and asked me a few questions. I don't even recall having to fill out an application, but in a matter of two days, I was scheduled for two interviews. I was elated now that all I had to do was ace the interviews. I did a little research on the schools and prepared for the interviews as my mom had taught me to do. I went over the standard interview questions and went on the first interview. The first interview didn't go as well as I hoped, but I still had one more opportunity to get the position. So the next day, I went to Milford Mill Academy and sat down for an interview. The principal was so welcoming and pleasant and so was the head of the business department. They seemed interested in what I had to say and enjoyed hearing about my journey to education. By the end of that interview, I was offered the job and would start the next day.

Since then, my career has grown as a result of me seeking out knowledge and empowering myself in preparation for the next phase. I constantly instill in my students that knowledge is power and the moment they stop being ignorant and enticed by the materialistic things in the world and the things around them, they will possess all the power they need to make it in life. My power lies in knowing who I am in Christ. Knowing that I am nothing without Him is essential, but also knowing that God can do nothing through me without my willing participation is just as important. I have to put forth an effort to do the things that I am instructed to do. At first it's hard to listen to a voice inside of you. You often wonder if you're going crazy or if what you are hearing is real. I have been able to understand the difference, but this only came with time, discipline, and maturity.

Reflection: Your Inner Voice

It's funny how we have our own agenda, which sometimes doesn't line up with God's agenda, or so we think. We want the quick and fast way to get to the end of the road, and God chooses the MOST unusual ways for us to travel. This is often how my life has been. When I was a teenager, I was so convinced that I could figure things out on my own, but God knew differently. He knew that I would need His guidance to learn important lessons that would lead me in the direction where He was taking me. I have always wanted to be a CEO and run an organization. I always wanted to be my own boss, and I knew I couldn't always work for someone else. As such, I assumed that I would graduate from college, attain a grand job in the business sector, and work my way up the ladder. Ha! What a joke! God knew that idea was way too small for what He had purposed me for in life, and it is evident that my plan didn't work out. So often, we spend too much of our time fulfilling our own agendas when we don't take time to ask God for His agenda. See His agenda, once I got on board with it, was so much easier to follow than my own. All I had to do was trust Him and follow directions.

It's like when you are traveling to a place that you have never been to before. The first thing you do is plug the directions into the navigation on your phone or in your car. You can't see the person talking to you, but you trust that the technology has been created to figure out all the ways in which you can get to your destination. You look at the directions and you know the area where the navigation is taking you. You think you know a better way that can get you there a little faster, thinking that the system just didn't consider this way because it's a smaller road and a much more discrete path. Once you start to detour, you find out that your way has construction and backups for hours. Now you go back to your GPS to see if it can get you out of the traffic jam and to your destination as soon as possible. You finally get there, but because of your detour it took you thirty minutes longer than what the system initially told you it would take to arrive.

This analogy is much like my life. It was hard to trust the process and route God was taking me on because I couldn't see Him and sometimes couldn't even hear Him. However, I found that life is so much easier when you just get connected to God and follow His plan. Using my logical mind oftentimes failed me, and I didn't obtain the outcome that I desired. Even though God's way put me in positions that I never planned, the results of being in His will were so rewarding and fulfilling. Just because you don't like the process, it doesn't mean you won't like the outcome.

So what path have you taken that you feel has ended in disaster? Where did things go wrong for you? Is it the decision to marry that guy or to take an unfulfilling job that offered you lots of money? What is it?

The Material Girl

God has a roadmap for each one of us and to find out what that is you have to begin hearing from Him. This seems weird for someone who has never once tried to hear from God, seen the need to hear from Him, and who has always thought that God only listens. We are created in His image and His likeness and that means we resemble Him. So if we have the capacity to speak and hear, so does God. Exercising this ability is similar to the practical notion of "use it or lose it." The more you purpose in your heart to seek out what He has for you, the more you'll find yourself hearing from Him.

List everything you are uncertain about in your life and the decisions you made that you believe have led you to an unhappy place. Once you make that list, pray to God that He shows you how to fix these areas (by calling them out) and ask Him for guidance and wisdom. **Proverbs 4:7-9** states, *"Wisdom is the principal thing; Therefore, get wisdom. And in all your getting, get understanding. Exalt her (wisdom), and she will promote you; She will bring you honor, when you embrace her. She will place on your head an ornament of grace; A crown of glory she will deliver to you."*

This passage as well as Proverbs chapter 2 have been my guiding light to navigating through life. I make it my mission to gain understanding in all things. The clarity that God gives can make you seem brilliant in a room full of CEOs—even when you're just the janitor. The wisdom and knowledge of God is the most powerful thing one can possess while on earth. I challenge you for the next month to read a new chapter from the book of Proverbs. Now these chapters are way shorter than a book chapter and should take you all of five minutes to read. For those new to the bible, start by using the Message or New King James versions. After you read each day's chapter, reflect and write down your interpretation of what it means or how you can relate the chapter to your life. Do this every day for at least thirty-one days. At the end of that period, journal your takeaways, including what you learned about God, and more importantly, note any changes you notice in yourself. This exercise will start you on a path that will uplift your spirit and create change.

Go to the back of the book to find the "Proverbs 31" Journal section. You can use this space to journal your reflections on the book of Proverbs for the next thirty-one days.

The Material Girl

Chapter 10
My Helper!

I'll never forget the day he prayed for me! I was at church sitting in the congregation like every other Sunday listening to my pastor teach. By this time it was fall of 2006, I was out of college and I recently started working my full-time job in Baltimore County. My life was really going well. I had recently started exclusively dating an older guy named Carlton who had a job, his own place, and treated me well. The pastor started to talk about fornication and the dire consequences that came from it. I had been around for a while and had heard some of this before. I knew it was a sin to have sex before marriage, but I still struggled with not engaging in sex with my boyfriend or whoever my exclusive partner was at that time. *Everyone else was doing it, so why couldn't I? It was the norm and God would forgive me... I mean isn't that what He's in the business of doing anyway?*

I could endure my pastor's rants about sex, but for some reason, on this day, he went in a totally different direction than I had expected. He went on to talk about getting pregnant as one of the consequences of pre-marital sex and how so many had turned to abortion as a way to escape their bad decisions. He talked about it

The Material Girl

being a sin and the turmoil it brings. It had been at least five years since I had talked about the abortion and at least a year since I had even thought about it. At that very moment, my eyes widened and a feeling a nausea made my stomach turn. I was reliving it all over again—the moment I found out I was pregnant, the moment I realized I was lost, and the time that made me change the trajectory of my life. *God why is this coming up again?* I thought to myself. *I thought if I confessed my sins, I would no longer have to deal with the guilt and pain.*

My pastor then proceeded to say he wanted to pray for all those who had abortions, so he told everyone dealing with the shame and hurt that lingered to come to the altar. Now I was no stranger to coming to the altar, but I was pissed. I wanted to grab my belongings and go. I thought I was cool. If it wasn't for him bringing it up, nothing lingered nor had I even thought about the child until he just mentioned it. I went back and forth with emotions of anger, fear, and sadness. I was sinking lower and lower in my seat. I dealt with this matter so much in private that my mom, at that time, still didn't know and Lord knows I was thankful that she wasn't there to find out. No one knew about the abortion, but a handful of people. Now the pastor wants me to stand up in front of a room full of 200 to 300 people for him to pray for me. Ummm, I'll past! As soon as I made the decision to stay seated, I heard from God. "Get up and go!" Before I could even fight the urge any longer, water was spilling out of my glassy eyes and running down my cheek. My vision was distorted and I could no longer see my surroundings. I got up and went to the altar trying to find my way. I got there and cried. I could not stop it. It was as if the pain was seeping out of my tears as I stood hunched over with my hands lifted. I couldn't understand why, why now? For all these years I hadn't shed one tear about this. Why now after I'd figured things out and started a new path. The altar was filled with women, both young and matured. Pastor started to pray for our pain to end and for us to forgive ourselves. He then walked to each person to lay hands on us, one by one he placed his hand on our heads.

    I could hear his voice but could not see him any longer, because my eyes were full of tears. As he laid his hands on my head, he stopped, placed both hands on my head, one at the top of my left ear and one over my right. He then whispered to me, "You can't live and do life like everyone else!" This word pushed me over. I was weeping out loud in an uncontrollable way, eyes closed shut, hand over my stomach in pain. I never will forget that day. His words rang in my ears for days to come. I didn't understand why. Why was my life so different? Why couldn't I live like everyone else my age? What did it all mean? I thought I was on a better path. *I just don't get it!* I thought.

    After that day, I decided to stop having sex. I wasn't sure how this would end, but I knew there was something different about my life that I had to obey. This journey was not easy at all. I was celibate for a year then started dating a new guy. I was too afraid or even embarrassed to tell the truth about my encounter, so I gave in, only to feel distraught and spiritually dead inside the next day. I did this for years, most of the time rekindling old flames because, I could not dare to be fornicating and promiscuous at the same time. Even while in a relationship at twenty-five and again at thirty, I tried to forget the moment when I was told that I couldn't live like that. It was hard because so often guys wouldn't understand. They would say things like, "God created sex!" "Does the bible really say that you couldn't have sex until marriage?" "The Man created the bible and there was a lot left out!" Or my favorite, "The white man created the constitution of marriage. That wasn't God!" I have found that you can't make your convictions someone else's and you can't

The Material Girl

convince someone of what you know in your heart and spirit. But what you know in your heart or spirit is how you are supposed to live.

After fruitless debates, I have decided to be okay with my choice without expecting the acceptance from anyone else. In this area, I have struggled to understand why, and constantly question whether I am being punished for my past. However, I have learned that maturity comes when you are okay living in your own skin and making God a priority. People will try to make you feel like the outcast or the one who is doing things wrong, but I was not created to be or act like anyone else, so I have become okay with being called different. While attending the bible institute, we learned about this thing called a "helper." Your helper leads and guides you to all truth—not man's truth or based on carnal understanding, but God's truth. The helper provides you with insight that most people never tap into which reveals wisdom beyond your comprehension. The key to this help is obedience! I had to first acknowledge what God had told me and how it aligned with my spirit. No one could understand the feelings I experienced within myself when I had sex. No one could tell me that what I was feeling wasn't true, because they didn't have the same feelings. Even when I tried to act like it was okay and forget about it, God would place representatives of the holy lifestyle He wanted me to live all around me. Either my pastor would happen to mention the turmoil that I was going through or I would read a sign that eluded to what I was hearing God speak to me. Whichever way it played out, those moments took me back to a mental place that confirmed God was real and reminded me to be obedient.

Although I wanted to just live life as I saw fit, there was a consistent pull to move me closer and closer to Him. I think what helped me the most was my eagerness not to be that seventeen-year-old (helpless) girl again. I knew I never wanted to feel empty again so I searched out as much as I could about what my pastor would say and what the bible said. The bible however tells us to avoid drunkenness (**Ephesians 5:18**) and even condemns it and its effects (**Proverbs 23:29-35**). The misnomer about the bible is that it is law. The bible is only a guide to living, not the complete package.

It's a book like any other informative book—in theory it can be likened to those that teach us how to create websites or build a home. These books may have been written ten years prior to you reading them, which makes them out of date, not extinct. You can read these books to learn the foundational principles to create a website or build a home, but things may have changed. Materials that existed when the book was written could be updated and codes for website features may now be solved by installing complete programs. Although the way these items are created and used are still the same, the materials and methods may be a little different. This is the same with the bible. It is said that it was created over 35,000 years ago and the conditions of that time are different from now. The key to it all is that the foundational principals are still the same, and God is the same yesterday, today, and forever more. We should read the bible to learn what happened, but also conduct our own research, including prayer, seeking personal revelation, and reading supplemental literature that may bring additional insight to a concept from the bible. It's sad that we live in a world where people would rather remain ignorant than to take the time to seek out the truth. The more I gain revelation through studying His word, the more He reveals His truth to me. It isn't enough to get saved. There is work attached to living a fulfilled lifestyle. Many might ask, "Why should I give up the things that make me happy or that I like to do if they don't hurt anyone?" The truth is that we don't realize how some of our actions (or sin committed against our bodies) end up revealing themselves in other areas of our lives.

The Material Girl

For instance, the act of drinking alcohol isn't a sin. Nowhere in the bible is that written. However, although being under the influence of alcohol feels euphoric, people's actions become unpredictable and it impairs many from using good judgement. Alcohol affects not only your actions but it also affects the brain and other bodily organs. Are you willing to cut your life short for a few hours of fun and the potential threat of becoming addicted to the numb feeling that alcohol creates? People do this every day, therefore our helper is an important part of our lives. When we have a direct line of communication with God, He can prevent us from doing things that would potentially create issues down the road. His ability to see beyond yours and my tomorrow is what makes the connection so important and vital.

The moment you tell people you "heard from God," they will try to question your understanding, especially if they themselves have never experienced it. In the beginning of your journey, I encourage you not to share those intimate moments with anyone at first. Just journal them down. You will find that over time, you will not care what anyone else thinks, because you will witness Him for yourself. Just try it! What do you have to lose? If you are already uncertain where your life is headed, have no clue of your purpose, and are drowning in debt trying to keep up with appearances, you don't have anything to lose. If you knew that reading a book could not only bring you wealth, but happiness and peace, would you read it? If your answer is "yes" to that question, open the bible and start reading. Confess this prayer believe in your heart, and start your journey. I have given you tools to start the process. Please note that every day will not be flowers and sunshine. The devil will try his best to detour you from the truth. Push through and believe in Him and watch how He will work in your life.

What You Wear Can't Conceal Who You Are

Romans 10:9-10 The Message (MSG)

The earlier revelation was intended simply to get us ready for the Messiah, who then puts everything right for those who trust him to do it. Moses wrote that anyone who insists on using the law code to live right before God soon discovers it's not so easy—every detail of life regulated by fine print! But trusting God to shape the right living in us is a different story—no precarious climb up to heaven to recruit the Messiah, no dangerous descent into hell to rescue the Messiah. So what exactly was Moses saying?

The word that saves is right here, as near as the tongue in your mouth, as close as the heart in your chest.

It's the word of faith that welcomes God to go to work and set things right for us. This is the core of our preaching. Say the welcoming word to God— "Jesus is my Master"—embracing, body and soul, God's work of doing in us what he did in raising Jesus from the dead. That's it. You're not "doing" anything; you're simply calling out to God, trusting him to do it for you. That's salvation. With your whole being you embrace God setting things right, and then you say it, right out loud: "God has set everything right between him and me!"

Prayer of Salvation:

Romans 10:9 states that if I confess Jesus as Lord and believe in my heart that God raised Jesus from the dead I shall be saved. So today I confess my belief in the savior and turn away from my carnal ways. I ask God that you will send your helper to guide me to your truth and lead me to understand your purpose and plan for my life. I pray the devil cease from his attacks on my body and my mind and commit to fight the good fight of faith. It is done in your Son Jesus' name, I have prayed. Amen!

The Material Girl

The key to this prayer is not just speaking it out loud but believing in the words you speak and consistently reminding yourself that God has the power over all things on earth.

Reflection: Wisdom

In the previous chapter, I suggested for you to read a Proverb for thirty-one days. You'll find that Proverbs speaks to the wisdom of God and you will hear wisdom cry out to you. Wisdom is your helper, the wisdom of God is that inward part that speaks the truth beyond your comprehension and understanding. At times, some things will make no logical sense, but you will have the foresight of God. Understanding this principal is not only hard for most, but also frightening. Some would even say it's just plain ole crazy. *If I hear voices, it must mean I'm crazy.* Well it all depends on what voices you are hearing. God's wisdom isn't a voice telling you to commit some heinous crime, but a small voice telling you to get up and write your business plan or give that homeless person $5 instead of the $1 you intended to give him. Holy Spirit is subtle, yet bold enough to have you do and say things that you would have never done on your own. The more you are aware that your helper exists, the more you will hear Him. The reading in Proverbs is crucial to this understanding. With the wisdom of God, comes knowledge and with the knowledge of God, you gain power. The power to have God's insight is the power to overcome troubling situations, to reach heights you couldn't have imagined, and to have dreams come true- Please note that the devil is a spirit as well, so understanding how God works and having the wisdom of God will help you determine the difference between the helper and the devil. .

What You Wear Can't Conceal Who You Are

For me it started with first reading His word and understanding how it applied to my life. Next, I acknowledged the power of God, then I prayed for understanding and insight, and lastly I activated faith to believe in His ability over my own. Holy Spirit is one of those topics that is hard for most people to understand. In a world where everything is accessible at the touch of your fingers, it seems unrealistic. I promise you, knowing the "helper" is the most beneficial tool to have while living on earth. In order to understand this concept more, you have to actually practice hearing.

The Material Girl

His Voice
(What is God speaking to you?)

Chapter 11
The War Isn't Over

As I mentioned before, after that March of 2001, I was on a search to find myself and figure out my purpose on earth. I had succumbed to such a big identity crisis that I had nowhere to turn, but to God for answers. At that time, I made a demand on God and asked Him "Why am I here?" After that, day-by-day He chipped away at the pieces of me that could not sustain with my purpose and unveiled key pieces to my puzzle. Everything building on the heel of another, some tests I passed and some I failed miserably. Nevertheless, I never stopped stepping up to the plate and taking on every challenge He placed before me. The clever thing about God is that He knew. He knew exactly what I would need to equip me for the next stages of my life. The bible tells us, in Ephesians 6, to put on the armor of God, prepare for a battle not of flesh, but spirit:

*Finally, my brethren, be strong in the Lord and in the **power** of His might. Put on the whole armor of God, that you may be able to stand against the wiles of the devil. For we do not wrestle against flesh and blood, but against principalities, against powers, against the rulers of the darkness of this age, against spiritual hosts of wickedness in the heavenly places. Therefore take up the whole* armor of God, that you may be able to **withstand in the evil day**, and having done all, to stand. Stand therefore, having girded your waist with **truth**, having put on the breastplate of **righteousness,** and having shod your feet with the **preparation** of the gospel of peace; above all, taking the shield of **faith** with which you will be able to quench all the fiery darts of the wicked one. And take the helmet of salvation, and the sword of the **Spirit**, which is the **word of God**; **praying** always with all prayer and supplication in the Spirit, being watchful to this end with all perseverance and supplication for all the saints— (**Ephesians 6:10-18 NKJV**)

    The words in bold are important! As I've stated throughout this book, I want all my readers to walk away with a better understanding of who God is in them. Everyone is different, but God is the same. He wants us all to walk in His power, but first we must commit to doing some things for Him. It's like trying to be on a basketball team, but in order to get in the game, the coach wants to know you can bring home a win. So you practice—you practice on your strength, your endurance, your skills, and your ability to work with others. These skills become vitally important when playing against a team with more experience than you. This is similar to God. Although everyone qualifies for the team, you first have to perfect your skills. Knowing He is Lord is not enough. You need to know how to fight against the devil when things come up in your life that challenge your faith and sometimes your livelihood. We are constantly in war with ourselves. Most say, "I can be my worst enemy!" which is true when you are unequipped and ill prepared for a war and enemies that have been assigned to your life.

    Even though the battle is won, your fight is continuous. This is important to grasp. I often heard people say, "The battle is already won," as if to suggest that by hearing those words, the enemy would just stop bothering us. However, that couldn't be farther from the truth. Becoming a believer, and a committed one, is just more reason for the enemy to continue fighting you. The devil won't rest until he has killed every part of you. The issue that causes you the most pain and trouble is what he will constantly use to torture you. Whether that issue is acceptance, lust, anger, greed, money—no matter what it is—don't think that just because you overcame one area that the battle is over.

    Although the church is a place to receive insight into what God says, that doesn't mean every church gives its members the truth about God's word. It's crazy how we hear things in church and don't take the time to examine its validity or its accuracy. During this time of slowly falling into what I call the devil's hands, I decided to read into the church saying (and what I thought was scripture), "The battle is already won." If the battle was already won, I wondered, why doesn't the devil leave me alone and why do I feel like I'm always fighting? If the battle is won, then that means there is no need to fight, right? However, God showed me something during this time of exploration and uncovering. Just because I have won one battle doesn't mean there won't be another one to fight. In the Old Testament, there is a story about Jehoshaphat, the King of Judah and Jerusalem in 2 Chronicles 20. This story is remarkable and seems unbelievable at times. Jehoshaphat was favored by God because he turned to Him for guidance. In the 20th chapter, Jehoshaphat received word that three armies were on their way to take over his land and kill everyone in it. Now Jehoshaphat knowing he did not have the manpower to fight this battle alone turned to God. God spoke through Jahaziel, a man in the congregation, and told the king that God said to go up and meet them but not to worry because he would fight this battle for them. Jehoshaphat and all of Judah and Jerusalem worshipped God. Even as they marched to meet armies for battle they sang songs of praise. By the time they had arrived to the meeting place, the three armies had mistaken each other for Judah and Jerusalem and had killed themselves. The bible states, "As soon as they started shouting and praising, God set ambushes against the men of Ammon, Moab, and Mount Seir as they were attacking Judah, and they all ended up dead. The Ammonites and Moabites mistakenly attacked those from Mount Seir and massacred them. Then, further confused, they went at each other, and all ended up killed," **2 Chronicles 22-23 (MSG).**

This illustration shows how God works. He will fight your battles for you as long as you give them to Him. But you will not know how to or that He can if you are not one with the Spirit, gaining understanding, and fellowshipping with God in prayer. I never stop talking to God. Every day I ask for guidance or talk to Him about things that happen. I may even just be thanking Him for allowing me to live. That constant communication and belief in His ability makes life easier.

By the age of thirty, I thought I had overcome a lot of the issues I faced when I was seventeen, but as I mentioned, the devil is always around trying to suck you back in. So right after the relationship with Kevin, I was yet again dealing with loneliness, depression, and sexual lust. I didn't instantly open the bible and start reading chapters, because my mind was not in the state where I could receive anything I would have read. My heart had become cold and numb and my ears could hear the devil louder than I could hear God. I was slowly falling into a state of depression and comfortability. I had become comfortable not listening to God, but because I had dived in the word before the storm, my spirit was fighting against the worldly part of me. It was an internal struggle of tug of war and for a minute I thought the devil had finally won.

But I just threw myself into what I knew and that was to surround myself with things that were a reflection of God's presence and His word. I called on my church friends who I had been avoiding because I didn't want to tell them the truth. I hung out with them. I knew their obedience and lifestyle would help me through.

 I listened to old preaching tapes and watched every Godly show possible. I didn't listen to secular music for a while or watch any TV. I journaled and journaled and journaled again. I read motivational books like Sarah Jakes *Lost and Found*. I did any and everything that would remind me of who I was in God. Most of the times, I didn't feel like it and wanted to stay in that dark place, because it was less work. But I was miserable there. I couldn't find any peace or happiness in that state of mind. Mental disease is real and if you allow negative voices to become the loudest thing you hear, your actions will surely follow. I never stopped going to church all together, although some days I wouldn't get out of bed. There was still a piece of me in the initial place that made me feel at home at Spirit of Faith. Some believe that you don't have to go to church to be in right standing with God. This is not completely wrong, but it's an incomplete thought. We are the church, so we do not have to go to church to be led by the Spirit or to talk to God. However, the church is where most people learn how to walk with God. It was created the same way school has been created to teach children how to be better citizens and maneuver in a world full of opportunities. Even when you graduate from secondary school, learning doesn't stop. You find yourself in trainings on the job or graduate studies to perfect your craft. So just because I had learned a lot, I still had a need to consistently be refreshed in spiritual truth that I had forgotten. Since God has ordained people as preachers and teachers of His word, they have insight to areas that we as the congregation may not. When you remove yourself from a place that feeds the spirit part of you, because you don't have all the answers, it can create deficits in areas of your life. Two is more powerful than one, so where two or more come together, God is there and able to do more than with just one man alone. *For where two or three are gathered*

The Material Girl

together in My name, I am there in the midst of them. - **Matthew 18:20**

    If I had not taken on the responsibility to become a better person, I would not have ever written this book. My battles with materialism have helped me reach so many young girls who I encounter as an educator and mentor. I am constantly fighting for my peace and therefore I understand that the war consists of multiple battles. I am willing to fight with the power of God each and every day. Today I am not just holy, I'm whole! I am at a place where I understand the contribution that I am designed to make in the world and how to do it. I do not always hit the mark, but I always have comfort in knowing that He is with me always.

Reflection: You're a Champion!

    By the time you are reading this final reflection, I hope you have gained a better understanding of who you are and how important your life is to others around you. As we venture through this world, we experience life in a multitude of ways. There are times in life where things are great and everything is going well and other times when you feel like your life is falling apart. However, you control your own destiny and when you realize that the finer things in life are not based on what you wear or the things you possess, you find peace in knowing it is in His ability to keep you in troubled times.

    I've gone through so many experiences in my life that has gotten me to this point, where I am content. My story may not be the same as yours, but the nuggets that I have laid out on these pages can be applied to your life. In life things happen, but how you deal with those things, not only define your future but build your character. You can overcome any situation if you're willing to fight.

What You Wear Can't Conceal Who You Are

At this point, you have outlined your life experiences and how they may or may not have affected your present state, wrote down your pull list, thought of habits you need to die to daily, learned how to kill the weeds, found out you had an inner voice and a helper, and now you know that you are a champion. You now have all you need to make the adjustments to your life to become the girl or guy who has Godly material. You just have to work his principles and tap into your inner being. I won't lie, this won't be easy; change is never easy or fun, but the payoff is worth it.

When we are born, we are purposed for something and God doesn't give it to you the way you think you should have it. It seems like it's never in a pretty red bow or wrapped in that shiny wrapping paper. It is normally wrapped in newspapers that look dull and uninteresting. However, what is in the newspaper is far better than what is in the wrapping paper. God doesn't spend time on the outside as much as he does on the inside, because he understands the outside is temporary and will eventual wilt away. BUT! God knows what is inside that paper are the components you will use the most, need the most, and value the most. They will sustain you through bad weather and be your tools to use in unlikely situations.

Going through the process of writing *The Material Girl* helped me reinforce this principle. Our outsides can easily be dressed up but what is on the inside takes work. Nothing that is valuable is created overnight, so neither was I. When I think of this logically, the formation of diamonds come to mind. If you know the process, it is said to take billions of years for them to form and are normally found in clusters. They are formed deep within the earth's mantel, the layer between the earth's crush and super-heated core. In the unseen part of the earth, under intense pressure and weather, carbon becomes diamonds. Researchers believe that heat has to be at 2,700 degrees Fahrenheit and the weight of over 4,000 grown men standing on your foot. The diamonds don't just appear on the earth's surface, they erupt onto earth from volcanos and once the materials are cooled, the diamond fragments can be found hidden within its rocks and dirt. Understanding this process will give you insight into the process God initiates when He elevates you. This revelation gives me so much joy, not because I am a high quality diamond with great clarity, cut, and chevrons, but to know He is so thoughtful to take His time not only to create me, but to build me. Being developed by God never stops; He is always working on the inward parts of us to create clarity, purity, and consistency.

Over the course of writing this book, I have taken more time reading other books and watching sermon after sermon. Some of my favorite books are authored by Sarah Jakes and Kevin Hart. Now I know that seems like such an oxymoron, however both have demonstrated a level of tenacity that I needed to feel encouraged through this time of my life. I felt so unqualified to write a book about my journey that I often talked myself out of moving forward. I am confident in my ability to do the things I know I am good at, but writing isn't one of them. I hated reading and writing growing up and it is still one of my least favorite things to do. "So, God you want me to write a book????" There were multiple question marks that came with this assignment.

"How do I publish a book?"

"What exactly do I share with the readers?"

"Who is my message for?"

"Will it reach the masses?"

I teetered with His instructions. One minute I was motivated to jump and other times, I despised God for even placing this in me. I didn't think I had the confidence to make this happen. Through the doubt and above all things, I trusted Him. He had gotten me through some tough times and how could I not believe that He would make things happen for me? I had no clue how I would make this work, but I did the only thing I knew how to do, research. I started investing my money into this book versus things. I took a class in writing, started to talk to my friends who I knew were writers, began following everyone I came across who God told me to watch, and lent my ears and eyes to anything that would push me to be a writer.

So in this last reflection, write down your goals and aspirations in life and what you learned from this book. Remember all the tools I have provided and the clarity that you have received in different areas of your life. How will you beat the odds and overcome the haters, doubt, and insecurities? You created a plan earlier. Now you have to explain how you will execute that plan to become a CHAMPION!

The Material Girl

Champion

Proverbs 31 Journal

Use the next 31 pages to journal your thoughts after reading a chapter of Proverbs a day.

Proverbs 1

Proverbs 2

Proverbs 3

Proverbs 4

Proverbs 5

Proverbs 6

Proverbs 7

Proverbs 8

Proverbs 9

Proverbs 10

Proverbs 11

Proverbs 12

Proverbs 13

Proverbs 14

Proverbs 15

Proverbs 16

Proverbs 17

Proverbs 18

Proverbs 19

Proverbs 20

Proverbs 21

Proverbs 22

Proverbs 23

Proverbs 24

Proverbs 25

Proverbs 26

Proverbs 27

Proverbs 28

Proverbs 29

Proverbs 30

Proverbs 31

About the Author

Mudiwa Noel is an author, educator, and mentor for girls. Her passion is to inspire youth to pursue their passions and develop an entrepreneurial mindset. She has received business and education degrees from Morgan State University, Trinity Washington University, and is pursuing a doctorate in education from Notre Dame of Maryland University. She has been a business educator in the Baltimore school system for over a decade and is dedicated to enriching the lives of young people.

Did you like The Material Girl?
Be sure to leave a review on Amazon.com and visit Mudiwanoel.com to subscribe to email updates and join Mudiwa at an upcoming event in your city.

www.ingramcontent.com/pod-product-compliance
Lightning Source LLC
Chambersburg PA
CBHW051059160426
43193CB00010B/1251